Fiqh us-Sunnah

FIQH us-SUNNAH

az-Zakāh and as-Siyām

'Abdul-Majid Khokhar
Muhammad Sa'eed Dabas
Jamal al-Din M. Zarabozo
(Translators)

American Trust Publications

© American Trust Publications 1410/1991

Published by American Trust Publications
2622 East Main Street
Plainfield, Indiana 46168-2703
Telephone (317) 839-8150
Fax (317) 839-2511

First Print 1991
Reprinted 1993
Reprinted 1997

Library of Congress cataloging in publication data
A catalog record for this book is available from the
Library of Congress

ISBN 0-89259-0 66-1

فَلَا وَرَبِّكَ لَا يُؤْمِنُونَ حَتَّىٰ يُحَكِّمُوكَ
فِيمَا شَجَرَ بَيْنَهُمْ ثُمَّ لَا يَجِـدُوا
فِي أَنفُسِهِمْ حَرَجًا مِمَّا قَضَيْتَ وَيُسَلِّمُوا تَسْلِيمًا .

But no, by your Lord!
They do not really believe
unless they make you
(O Prophet) a judge
of all on which they disagree
among themselves,
and then find in their hearts
no bar to an acceptance
of your decision
and give themselves up to it
in utter self-surrender (an-Nisa' 4:65).

Part I az-Zakāh

O you who believe! Shall I lead you to a bargain that will save you from grievous suffering [in this world and in the life to come]?

You are to believe in Allah and His Messenger and strive hard in Allah's cause with your possessions and your lives: this is for your own good – if you had known it (as-Saff: 10-11).

[O Muhammad!] also mention [to them] in the Book [the story] of Ishma'il: He was always true to his promise, and he was a messenger [of Allah] and a prophet, who enjoined upon his people prayer and *zakāh*, and found favor in his Sustainer's sight (Maryam: 54).

And remember We took a covenant from the children of Israel: Worship none but Allah; treat with kindness your parents and relatives and orphans and the destitute; speak fair to the people; be steadfast in prayer; and give *zakāh*. Then did you turnback, except a few among you ... (al-Baqarah: 83).

He [Jesus] said: "I am indeed a servant of Allah. He has given me revelation and made me a prophet; and he has made me blessed wherever I be, and has enjoined upon me prayer and *zakāh* as long as I live" (Maryam: 30).

CONTENTS

PREFACE

This volume consists of two parts: *az-zakāh* and *as-siyām*. For *az-zakāh*, we commissioned more than one translator because of the technical nature of the subject and its complexity. Out of the three versions we selected 'Abdul-Majid Khokhar's translation for its smooth and true rendition.

For *as-siyām* and *i'tikāf*, we relied upon our original team of Muhammad Sa'eed Dabas and Jamal al-Din Zarabozo. In both cases the final version was prepared by the editors of the American Trust Publications. If there is any merit in the present work, the credit goes to the translators and not to us. However, we stand responsible for any textual and syntax problem. May Allah *subhanhu wa ta'la* reward all of them for their contribution to this work.

Publishers

OF ZAKAH AND SADAQĀT

Throughout this work, the words *sadaqah* and *zakah* have been used interchangeably which might cause confusion in some of our readers' mind. The reason for such confusion is obvious: if *sadaqah* and *zakah* are the same, then why not stick to one term. On the other hand, if the two vary in meaning, then why not use their precise application according to the text's demands? As such, a little explanation is due.

Linguistically, *sadaqah* is derived from the root *sadq* or *sidq*, which means "to speak the truth, to be sincere." It can also mean, "candor and efficiency." The Qur'ānic lexicon transfigures this verbal root into *sadaqah* — a term applicable to the concept of a gift offered to someone from one's rightfully owned holdings without regret or remorse or without any ulterior motives, in short, for the pleasure of Allah, the Exalted. It therefore partakes of four essential elements: legitimacy of one's holdings, sincerity of intention, altruistic motives, and the condition that it is for Allah alone.

At first glance, sincerity of intention, altruism, and seeking Allah's pleasure may strike a case of redundancy. However, the three are interdependent. For example, a person could be sincere in helping others, he could also be motivated by altruism. Still, the two would not endow it with the character of a *sadaqah* because of one missing ingredient — that is, giving it for Allah alone. This is so because *sadaqah* is not an exclusive concept. Rather, it is embedded in the eschatology of Islam which paradoxically includes the concerns of this life as well. Not surprisingly, the Qur'ān refers to the giving of *sadaqāt* as an essential component of its program for mankind. While giving the oath of allegiance (*bai'ah*) to Muhammad, *sallal lahu alehi wasallam,* the companions used to promise that they would, among other things, spend in the way of Allah – whether they were rich or poor. 'Ubādah ibn Samit's *hadith* is pertinent to the point:

> The Messenger of Allah, *sallalahu alehi wasallam,* took our oaths of allegiance [on the points] that we would abide by him under all circumstances, that in richness as well as in poverty we will spend in the way of Allah, that we will enjoin goodness and forbid evil, and that we will tell the truth for Allah with least regard to consequences.

Why *sadaqat* were tied in the *bai'ah* is a question worth pondering. Though voluntary by nature, the promise to give *sadaqat* was an essential part of the oath because, without such an undertaking, the new community could not have survived even its first test. *Sadaqāt* symbolized in a meaningful way the solidarity and brotherhood among the members of the Muslim ummah. They provided a safety net for the newly initiated who were alienating themselves from their *kafir* society and thus facing economic hardships. Limiting it to a specified amount would have been damaging to the very concept by vitiating its voluntary character. At the same time, it would have denied the community the vast resources that it garnished for its need through *sadaqāt.* Last, it would have retarded the spiritual and moral growth of its members which the promise of Islam held for them. It is peculiar to the spirit of Islam that it took upon itself the reconstruction of a new society where the poor were not to be despised or ignored, and where people felt bound to each other because they cared.

This kind of social realignment necessarily originated in the Islamic concept that God is compassionate and Who, in the eloquent words of the Qur'ān, *"kattabā rab-bukum 'ala naf si hir-rahmah,"* has taken upon Himself mercy for the believers. The divine virtue therefore had to be reflected in the believers' character. *Sadaqat* provided not only a catharsis for the individual sense of guilt toward the deprived but they also imparted a sense of achievement to the giver that he was a partner in the collective effort to usher in a new dawn.

Thus, *sadaqāt* had to go beyond the meaning of charity or beneficence. Even though giving away money was its most potent expression, it never stayed imprisoned in its material mold; it stretched itself to become a style of life – a new paradigm. That is why, according to the *ahadith*, a *sadaqah* could be anything. Size, amount, or form is immaterial. A flicker of smile that comes on a believer's face at the sight of another believer or his removal of any hazardous material from a road is as valuable as a big donation could be.

In a very remarkable *hadith*, Abu Musa al-Ash'ari reported Allah's messenger, upon whom be peace, as saying that every Muslim must give *sadaqah* (charity). He [the Messenger] was asked how this could apply to one who had nothing, and he replied that he should work with his hands, gaining benefit for himself thereby and giving *sadaqah*. Asked what would happen if a person was unable to do this or did not do it, the Messenger replied that he should help one who is in need and sad. Asked what he should do if he did not do that, he replied that he should enjoin what is good. Asked what he should do if he did not do that, he replied that he should refrain from evil, for that would be *sadaqah* for him.[1]

What matters in such cases is the intention. If it is for Allah, then it falls within the ambit of worship. Paradoxically, it does not assume the character of an obligation, even though in some ways, its reward defies any time frame and continues benefitting the doer as long as his *sadaqah* has validity to life. For example, the construction of a school or the raising of a good Muslim family survives the dead and any good accrued on them benefits the dead. This is strikingly different from prayer (*salah*) and fasting (*siyām*) which because of its esoteric nature go with the deceased at the time of death.

On the other hand, *zakah* is a *sadaqah* of a compulsive nature which the rich have to pay to an Islamic state in order to help it create an economically conducive environment where its citizenry could live in love and friendship and whereby it could realize its ideological imperatives. In other words *zakah*, in its broad scope, deals with the fiscal policies of a state as it affects its moral and spiritual climate – a vehicle for social change, a source of its continuity, and a device for the safeguard of its ideological frontiers in a world not very friendly. In the hands of the Prophet, *sallalahu alehi*

---

[1]*Sahih al-Bukhari, Sahih Muslim, Mishkat-al-Masabih,* vol. 1, p. 403.

wasallam, zakah proved to be a most effective tool, one he used imaginatively to build the Islamic movement, win over its enemies to its cause, and spread its influence. To characterize *zakah* as an alms tax is not only to minimize its scope but to demean it. After all, the Qur'ān elevates *zakah* to the level of *salah* (a worship exclusively for Allah) and gives both an equation which, by all counts, remains unique in the Qurā'nic diction. The way it is collected, with no trace of oppression — allowing the individual to separate his goods for *zakah* on his own, restricting the collector to take whatever is given to him, and then in culmination making suplication (*dua'*) for the giver that his wealth may increase — imparts *zakah* with a character that goes far beyond that of a tax.

What is remarkable about *zakah* is that it finishes a job that taxation, to begin with, cannot accomplish. All taxation systems enacted by a state are marked by tension between the government and citizens. Whether such tension is expressed or not is beside the point. The fact is that it is there. Even in the so-called advanced societies where the role of taxation in the modern-day state is very well understood, there is a perennial conflict of interests between the tax giver and the recipient. The question "Why should I support social programs?" continues popping up in different forms and debates.

Zakah does not carry such problems because it does not ignore the human context of economic relations. It is man who is at the heart of its program. 'Alijah 'Ali Izetbegovic has brought out this point very eloquently when he said:

> Every social solution must include a human solution. It should change not only economic relations, but also the relations between men. It should bring about the just distribution of goods as well as proper upbringing, love, and sympathy.
>
> Poverty is a problem, but it is also a [social] sin. It is not solved only through a shift in the ownership of goods, but also through personal striving, aim, and goodwill. Nothing would be done in the true sense of the word if there were change in the ownership of the goods, but hatred, exploitation, and subjugation remained in men's souls. This is the reason for the failure of Christian religious revolts and socialist revolutions.[2]

---

[2]'Alijah 'Ali Izetbegovic, *Islam Between East and West,* (Indianapolis: American Trust Publications, 1984), pp. 160, 161.

So great is Islam's concern for the poor and the needy that when the system fails to obtain results or when those who are well-offs are unresponsive to the deprived, the latter are given permission to snatch their needs from the former − especially in a situation of hunger. This kind of radicalism is peculiar to Islam which cannot be explained in socialistic jargons or condemned in bourgeois concerns for law and order. It is man and his right to live which overrules everything else.

Sayyid Sabiq's preference of the term *zakah* for the *'id*-dues, though acceptable within *fiqhi* literature, is not technically beyond dispute.

In *ahadith* dealing with *sadaqat ul-fitr*, the word *zakat ul-fitr* has also been used − perhaps to stress its obligatory nature.

> The Prophet, upon whom be peace, made incumbent on every male or female, free man or slave, the payment of one *sa'* of dates, or barley, as *zakat ul-fitr* (or said *sadaqah Ramadān*).[3]

In another *hadith*, Ibn 'Abbas narrates: The Prophet enjoined *sadaqat ul-fitr* so that those who observed fasting are purified of their indecent and shameful errors, and so the poor and the needy ones are enabled to arrange for their basic necessities of food and clothing. Thus, the *sadaqah* of the person who gives it before the *'id* prayer will be accepted by Allah as *zakat ul-fitr*, but the *sadaqah* of the one who delays and pays it afterwards will be treated as an ordinary charity.[4]

Four principles can be derived from the preceding hadith:

✔ *Sadaqat ul-fitr* (*'id*-due) is obligatory on all.
✔ Its payment purifies the giver of his bad deeds, and thus, perfects his fasting.
✔ Its purpose is to help the poor and the needy to rejoice in the *'id*.
✔ Its early payment brings great rewards.

---

[3]*Sahih al-Bukhari*, p. 342

[4]Ibn Dawud, Ibn Majah

Some jurists, though, concede the obligatory nature of *sadaqat ul-fitr*, nevertheless, qualifies it with the possession of *nisab*. Thus, if a person on the morning of *'id* does not have the minimum amount that makes him liable to pay *zakah,* then he is not bound to pay *sadaqat ul-fitr.* The others hold that the possession of *nisab* is not the prerequisite. Any person who possesses a day's provision has to pay *sadaqat ul-fitr.* Three arguments can be offered in favor of the latter view:

- ✓ In almost all *ahadith* on the subject, the precondition of *nisab* is not there.
- ✓ The amount to be paid is very small – that is, 2176 grams of dates, barley, wheat or any other food item available, in kind or value.
- ✓ The characteristics of *zakah,* tied to *nisab,* are not found in *sadaqat ul-fitr.* For example, *zakah* is not incumbent upon children (without *nisab*), while the *sadaqat ul-fitr* is.

Besides, for the payment of *zakah,* the *zakah* year is to be completed while there is no such period for *sadaqat ul-fitr.* The parents will pay *sadaqat ul-fitr* even for a baby born before the dawn of *'id.*

A person who dies before the dawn of *'id* will be exempted from paying *sadaqat ul-fitr,* while in the case of *zakah,* if the person dies before the expiration of the *zakah* year and the *zakah* is due, it will be paid by the heirs.

Zakah, as an institution, is intimately tied to the fiscal policies and even plays a greater role in removing inequalities in society. Its application is not confined to a day or two but goes beyond a year. On the contrary, *sadaqat ul-fitr* are specifically meant for the *'id,* so that those who lack food or other means to rejoice the occasion, may not feel deprived on *'id.*

A passing reference can also be made to *zakah* on fruits and vegetables. In the classical literature on *zakah* as well as in the present work, items like vegetables and fruits, except grapes and dates, were excluded from zakah. The *ahadith* support such a *zakah* policy. However, if in such matters the intention of the *shar'iah* is crucial as a determinant, then a rationale can be built to find out why the Prophet, *sallalahu alehi wasallam,* excluded them from *zakah.*

There are two kinds of edibles: *muqtāt* (stable or nonperishable) and non-*muqtāt* (perishable). The Prophet subjected *muqtāt* items to *zakah* perhaps because of their relatively long storage life, while he left out perishable items. Vegetables and fruits obviously fell under this category. The only exception were grapes for which one can say that since they can be turned into raisins he subjected them to *zakah*, despite their being a fruit. If this kind of reasoning is acceptable, then it can be argued that with the refrigeration now possible, the distinction between perishable and nonperishable as determinant (if it ever was) for *zakah* is not tenable any more, especially in the case of apples, oranges, bananas, and peaches. Likewise, analogously with grapes which can be dried into raisins, a case can be built for apples, apricots, pineapples, and bananas as well. All these fruits can be dried and given a long storage life and could be *perhaps* subjected to *zakah*. Allah knows best.

M. Tariq Quraishi
Rajab 2, 1407

ZAKAH IN ISLAMIC
JURISPRUDENCE

Definition: *Zakah* or alms tax can be defined as that portion of a man's wealth which is designated for the poor. The term is derived from the Arabic verbal root meaning "to increase." "to purify," and "to bless." It finds its origin in Allah's command to: "Take *sadaqah* (charity) from their property in order to purify and sanctify them" [*at-Taubah*: 103]. That is why this kind of *sadaqah* is called *zakah*, for by paying it, one is aspiring to attain blessing, purification, and the cultivation of good deeds.

Taking into account its very nature, it is no wonder that *zakah* constitutes one of the five pillars of Islam. It is associated with prayer (*salah*) in eighty-two Qur'ānic verses. Allah, the Exalted One, pre-scribed it in His Book (The Qur'ān), His Messenger corroborated it by his (*sunnah*), and the community (*ummah*) by consensus upheld it. Ibn 'Abbas reported that when the Prophet, upon whom be peace, sent Mu'adh ibn Jabal to Yemen (as its governor), he said to him: "You are going to a people who are People of the Scripture. Invite them to accept the *shahadah*: that there is no god but Allah and I am His Messenger. If they accept and affirm this, tell them that Allah, the Glorious One, has enjoined five prayers upon them during the day and night. If they accept that, tell them also that He has enjoined *sadaqah* upon their assets which will be taken from the rich of the (Muslim) community and distributed to the poor. If they accept that, refrain

[1]

from laying hands upon the best of their goods and fear the cry of the oppressed, for there is no barrier between Allah and it."

At-Tabarani relates in *al-'Awsāt* and *as-Saghīr*, on the authority of 'Ali, that the Prophet said: "Allah has enjoined upon rich Muslims a due to be taken from their properties corresponding to the needs of the poor among them. The poor will never suffer from starvation or lack of clothes unless the rich neglect their due. If they do so, Allah will surely hold them accountable and punish them severely." According to at-Tabarani: "It was reported only by Thabit ibn Muhammad az-Zahid." Of Thabit's credibility, al-Hafiz in turn says: "Thabit was an honest and trustworthy person. Al-Bukhari and others related from him, and the rest of the narrators in the chain are considered as accepted authorities."

In the early days of Islam at Makkah, no limit or restriction was placed on the amount to be donated, for that decision was left to the individual Muslim's conscience and generosity. In the second year of *hijrah*, according to the widely known authorities, both the type and the quantity of *zakah* revenues were determined, and detailed illustrations were provided.

Exhortation to Give *Zakah*

(a) **From the Qur'ān:** *At-Taubah*: 103 authorizes the Prophet, upon whom be peace, to take either a stipulated amount of alms from the believers' holdings in the form of the obligatory *zakah*, or a voluntary, unstipulated amount (*zakah* of *tatawwu'*). In this *'ayah*, "purify" means to purify them from stinginess, greed, and meanness, and a lack of remorse toward the poor and the wretched. To sanctify them is to raise them in esteem through good deeds and blessings so that they will be worthy of happiness both now and in the afterlife.

In reference to the life hereafter, Allah reveals: "Lo! Those who keep from evil will dwell amid gardens and watersprings, taking that which their Lord gives them. For they were before doers of good. They used to sleep but little of the night, and in the hours of the early dawn they prayed for forgiveness. . . . In their wealth, the beggar and the outcast had due share" [*adh-Dhariyat*: 15-19]. Allah views beneficence and righteousness as exclusive qualities of the pious. It is because of their beneficence that they pray at night and ask Allah's forgiveness at dawn as a way of worshipping and approaching Him. Their beneficence is likewise in their giving to the needy their share of mercy and sympathy.

Allah further confirms: "And the believers, men and women, are protecting friends of one another; they enjoin the right and forbid the wrong, they perform prayer and pay the *zakah*, and they obey Allah and His Messenger. Upon them, Allah will have mercy" [*at-Taubah*: 71].

Such are the people blessed by Allah and given His mercy — those who believe in Him, who take care of each other through support and love, who exhort fairness and restrain lewd behavior, who have strong ties with Allah through prayer, and who strengthen their mutual relations through *zakah*.

Finally, these people, as reflected in *al-Hajj*: 41, are: "Those who, if we give them power in the land, perform prayers and pay *zakah*, and enjoin kindness and forbid inequity." Giving *zakah* is, therefore, one of the reasons for which the righteous are given authority on earth.

(b) From the Hadith: At-Tirmidhi relates from Abu Kabshah al-Anmari that the Prophet, upon whom be peace, said: "I swear upon three (things) and ask you to memorize my words: *Sadaqah* taken from a property never decreases it; a man who suffers injustice and is patient with it, Allah will grant him strength; a man who starts begging, Allah will cause him to be poor."

Ahmad and at-Tirmidhi relate (and the latter graded it *sahih*) from Abu Hurairah that the Messenger of Allah, upon whom be peace, said: "Allah receives charity by His right hand, and then He causes it to grow for each of you. Just as you raise a horse, colt, foal, or young weaned camel, so that morsel becomes as large as the Mount of 'Uhud."

Of this *hadith*'s content, Waki' says: "This is sanctioned by the Qur'an: 'Do they not know that it is Allah alone who can accept the repentance of His servants and is the (true) recipient of whatever is offered for His sake - and that Allah alone is an acceptor of repentance, a dispenser of grace?' [*at-Taubah*: 104]. 'Allah deprives usurious gains of all blessing, whereas He blesses charitable deeds with manifold increase.' [*al-Baqarah*: 276]."

Again, Ahmad relates, with a sound chain of narrators, that Anas said: "A man from the tribe of Tameem came to the Messenger of Allah, upon whom be peace, and said: 'O Messenger of Allah! I have plenty of property, a large family, a great deal of money, and I am a gracious host to my guests. Tell me how to conduct my life and how to spend.' The Messenger of Allah, upon whom be peace, replied: 'Pay *zakah* out of your property, for truly it is a purifier which purifies you, and be kind to your relatives, and acknowledge the rights of the poor, neighbors, and beggars'."

It was reported from 'Aishah that the Messenger of Allah, upon whom be peace, said: "I swear upon three things: Allah does not equate one who has a portion in Islam with one who does not. The portions of Islam are three: prayer, fasting, and *zakah*. If Allah takes care of a man in this world, He will take care of him on the Day of Judgment. If a man likes a group of people, Allah will certainly include him among them. As for the fourth, if I swear on it, I hope I will not commit a sin: that if Allah conceals a man's sin in this world, He will certainly not expose him on the Day of Judgment."

At-Tabarani relates in *al-'Awsāt*, that Jabir reported: "A man said: 'O Messenger of Allah! What will be the gains for a man who pays *zakah* on his assets?' The Messenger of Allah, upon whom be peace, said: 'For one who pays *zakah* on his asssets, he will be removed from the evil in them'."

On the same subject, al-Bukhari and Muslim relate that Jabir ibn 'Abdullah reported: "I gave my allegience to the Messenger of Allah, upon whom be peace, that I will establish *salah* (prayers) and *zakah*, and I will give advice to every Muslim."

Punishment for the Delinquents of *Zakah*

(a) From the Qur'an: Allah says: "O you who believe! Most surely many of the doctors of law and the monks eat away the property of men falsely and turn them from Allah's way; and as for those who hoard treasures of gold and silver and do not spend them for the sake of Allah — warn them of grievous sufferings [in the life to come]. On the Day when that [hoarded wealth] shall be heated in the Fires of Hell and their foreheads and their sides and their backs branded with it, [it will be said to them:] 'These are the treasures which you have hoarded for yourselves. Now taste of what you used to accumulate!' [*at-Taubah*: 34-35]." He also says: "And they should not think — they who avariously cling to all that Allah has granted them out of His bounty — that this is good for them. No, it is bad for them, for that which they hoard will be hung about their necks on the Day of Judgment" [*al-'Imran*: 180].

(b) From the *Hadith*: Ahmad, al-Bukhari, and Muslim relate from Abu Hurairah that the Messenger of Allah, upon whom be peace, said: "No owner of a treasure who does not pay *zakah* will be spared, for his treasure will be heated in the Fires of Hell and then made into plates. His flanks and his forehead will be branded with them until Allah pronounces judgment on His servants during a day lasting fifty thousand years.

[The individual] will be shown his path, leading him either to Paradise or to Hell. A camel owner who does not pay *zakah* will not be spared (either). He will lay flat on a sandy, soft plain and they will run over him heavily one after another until Allah pronounces judgment on His servants during a day lasting fifty thousands years. [The individual in question] will then be shown his path, leading him either to Paradise or to Hell. Equally, no owner of goats who does not pay *zakah* (will be spared). He will lay flat for them on a sandy plain, and the goats will run over him as heavy as they will come and they will trample him with their hoofs and gore him with their horns — with twisted horns or with no horns — one after another until Allah pronounces judgment on His servants, during a day lasting fifty thousand years, and [the individual in question] will be shown the path, leading him either to Paradise or to Hell. They [the Companions] asked: 'O Messenger of Allah, what about the horses?' He said: 'Horses have goodness in their foreheads (or he said 'Goodness lies in the foreheads of the horses') until the Day of Judgment. Horses are of three kinds: they are a source of reward for the owner, they are a cover, or they are a burden to a person. As to those [horses] that bring rewards, one who raises and trains them for the sake of Allah will get a reward from Him as well as all that they consume will be considered a reward for him from Allah. For every stalk of grass in the meadow that one lets them graze, there is a reward for him. For every drop of water that one lets them drink from the creek, there is a reward.' He went on describing until a reward was mentioned even for their urine and their feces.

'And for every step that they prance on elevated ground, there is a reward. As for the one to whom they will provide cover [in the life hereafter], he is the one who raises them for honor and dignity and remembers the right of their backs and stomachs in plenty and adversity. As for the one to whom they are a burden, he is the one who raises them for glory and showing off to people.' They asked: 'O Messenger of Allah, what about donkeys?' He said: 'Allah has not revealed to me anything in regard to them except this one comprehensive verse: 'He who does an atom's weight of good will see it, and he who does an atom's weight of evil will see it' [*az-Zalzalah*: 7]."

Al-Bukhari and Muslim relate from Abu Hurairah that the Prophet, upon whom be peace, said: "Whoever is made wealthy by

Allah and does not pay *zakah* on his wealth, on the Day of Judgment it will become a bald-headed, poisonous, male snake with two black spots over his eyes. The snake, on the Day of Judgment, will encircle his neck, and bite his cheeks and say: 'I am your treasure, I am your wealth.'" Then he [the Prophet] recited this *'ayah*: "'And let not those who hoard up that which Allah has bestowed upon them of his bounty...' [*al-'Imran*: 180]."

Ibn Majah, al-Bazzar, and al-Baihaqi relate from Ibn 'Umar that the Messenger of Allah, upon whom be peace, said: "O Muhajirun, beware of five traits: if ever immorality spreads in a community and there is no sense of shame on its occurrence or mentioning it [and people talk about it as if nothing bad has taken place], diseases which were not present in the time of their predecessors will spread among them. If they decrease the measure and weight (of sold grains or food), they will be overcome by poverty, their provisions will decrease and their ruler will be unjust. If they refrain from paying the *zakah* due on their properties, they will be deprived of rain, unless they get it only for the sake of their cattle. If they renounce their commitment to Allah and His Messenger, they will be governed by an enemy who is a stranger to them and who will take away some of what they possess. If their rulers do not rule according to Allah's Book, they will be afflicted by civil war. Allah forbid that these should happen to you."

Al-Bukhari and Muslim relate from al-Ahnaf ibn Qays that he said: "I was in the company of some men of Quraish, when a man (Abu Dharr al-Ghafari, a companion of the Prophet) came with coarse hair, clothes, and appearance. He stood up, greeted them and said: 'Inform those who hoard property that a stone will be heated in the Fires of Hell and then placed on the nipples of their breasts until it comes out from the top of their shoulders. It will then be placed on the top of their shoulders until it comes out again from the nipple of their breasts, and they will be shaken.' Then he left. I followed him and sat near him, not knowing who he was. I said: 'These people disliked what you said to them.' He observed: 'They do not understand anything that my friend said to me.' I asked: 'Who is your friend?' He replied: 'The Prophet, upon whom be peace. [One day he asked me]: 'Do you see the Mount of Uhud?' I looked at the sun to see how much of the day was left, as I thought that the Messenger of Allah, upon whom be peace, wanted to send me on an errand for him. I said: 'Yes.' Upon this he said: 'Nothing would delight me more than having gold equal to the bulk of Uhud and spending all of it (in Allah's way) except three *dinars*.'

'Indeed, these people do not understand and go on accumulating riches. By Allah! I neither ask them for this world, nor do I ask them anything about religion until I meet Allah, The Exalted One.' "

Judgment on the *Zakah* Refrainer

As an obligation upon Muslims, *zakah* is one of the essential requirements of Islam. If somebody disputed its obligation, he would be outside of Islam, and could legally be killed for his unbelief unless he was a new Muslim and could be excused for his ignorance.

As for the one who refrains from paying it without denying its obligation, he would be guilty of committing a sin. Yet, this act does not place him outside of Islam. It is the ruler's duty to take *zakah* from the defaulter by force and rebuke him, provided he does not collect more than the stipulated amount. However, in the views of Ahmad and ash-Shaf'i (in his earlier opinion) the ruler could take half of the defaulter's money, in addition to the calculated amount of *zakah*, as a punishment. This view is based on what Ahmad, an-Nasa'i, Abu Dawud, al-Hakim, and al-Baihaqi have recorded from Bahz ibn Hakim all the way back to his grandfather who said: "I heard the Messenger of Allah, upon whom be peace, say: 'Whether the camels of the *zakah* payer are grown or baby camels, it makes no difference in his reward if he gave them willingly. (However,) if someone refrains from paying it, it will be taken from him along with half his property, for it is a right of our Lord, the Blessed and the Exalted, not a right of the house of Muhammad.' "

Asked about its chain, Ahmad ruled it good (*hassan*). Of Bahz, al-Hakim says: "His traditions are authentic." Ash-Shaf'i, as al-Baihaqi says, did not include it for *fiqhi* consideration because ... "this *hadith* is not confirmed by the scholars of *hadith*."

If some people refrain from paying *zakah* knowing that it is due and that they can afford to pay, they should be fought until they yield and pay. Al-Bukhari and Muslim report that Ibn 'Umar heard the Prophet say: "I have been ordered to fight people until they say that none has the right to be worshipped but Allah, and that Muhammad is His Messenger, and they uphold the prayers, and pay the *zakah*. If they do this, their lives and properties will be safe, except for what is due to Islam, and their accounts are with Allah."

Abu Hurairah is reported to have said: "When Allah's Messenger, upon whom be peace, died and Abu Bakr succeeded him as caliph, some Arabs apostasized, causing Abu Bakr to declare war upon them. 'Umar said to him: 'Why must you fight these men?', especially when there is a ruling of the Prophet, upon whom be peace: 'I have been called to fight men until they say that none has the right to be worshipped but Allah, and whoever said it has saved his life and property from me except when a right is due in them, and his account will be with Allah.' Abu Bakr replied: 'By Allah! I will fight those who differentiate between *salah* and *zakah* because *zakah* is the due on property. By Allah! If they withheld even a young she-goat (*'anaq*) that they used to pay at the time of Allah's Messenger, upon whom be peace, I would fight them.' Then 'Umar said: 'By Allah! It was He who gave Abu Bakr the true knowledge to fight, and later I came to know that he was right.' "

The same *hadith* narrated by Muslim, Abu Dawud, and at-Tirmidhi has the following variant: "If they witheld the *'iqal*, the rope of the camel," instead of " '*anaq*, young she-goat."

Who is Obliged to Pay *Zakah*?

Zakah must be paid by every Muslim who has a *nisab*, which is the minimum of one's holdings liable to *zakah*. The *nisab* is conditioned by the following:

1) *Zakah* should be paid on any amount of money remaining after meeting the expenses for such necessities as food, clothes, housing, vehicles and craft machines.

2) A complete year of Islamic calendar should pass, starting from the very day of the *nisab*'s possession, without any decrease during the year. In case of its decrease (being less than *nisab*), the year count (*hawl*) starts from the day of the *nisab* completion.

Commenting on the issue, an-Nawawi said: "In our view and the views of Malik, Ahmad, and the majority of scholars, the amount of property liable for payment of *zakah*, such as gold, silver, or cattle, is tied to the completion of *nisab* through the turn of a whole year. If the *nisab* decreases in any time of the year, [the counting of] the year discontinues. Later, if the *nisab* is completed, the year count is resumed from the time of its completion."

On the same subject, Abu Hanifah holds: "What matters is the availability of *nisab* at the beginning and end of the year. Its decrease at any time in between does not matter, even though the *zakah* payer had two hundred *dirhams* and he lost all but one *dirham* during the year, or if he had forty sheep, all of which died except for one during the year. If, at the end of the year, he had two hundred *dirhams*, or forty sheep, then he must pay *zakah* on all of that. This condition is not applicable to the *zakah* of plantations and fruits, for their *zakah* should be paid on the harvest day. Allah, the Exalted One, says: 'And pay the due thereof upon the harvest day' [*al-A'raf*: 142]."

Al-'Abdari elaborated that: "The holdings subject to *zakah* are of two kinds. The first kind grows by itself: crops and fruits. The second kind is used for growing and production: money, merchandise, and cattle. In the former case, *zakah* should be paid at the time of harvest. In the latter case, it should be paid at the end of the *haul*. This was the opinion of all jurists as reported in an-Nawawi's *al-Majmu'*."

Zakah on the Holdings of Infants and Mentally Retarded People

The guardian of a child or of a mentally retarded person must pay *zakah* on his behalf from his property if it constitutes a *nisab*.

'Amr ibn Shu'aib reported from his father backed up by a chain of sources going back to 'Abdullah ibn 'Amr that the Messenger of Allah, upon whom be peace, said: "One who becomes the guardian of an orphan with property must trade on his behalf and not leave it passive in order to avoid depletion of the property by *sadaqah*."

However, this *hadith* has a weak link. Still, al-Hafiz affirms that: "There is a similar *hadith* of the *mursal* type in the compilation of ash-Shaf'i, who confirmed that it is considered a sound one. 'Aishah used to set aside *zakah* for the orphans who were under her protection."

At-Tirmidhi concludes that: "Jurists differ on this issue. More than one companion of the Prophet, upon whom be peace, said that *zakah* may be taken from an orphan's property. Among these are: 'Umar, 'Ali, 'Aishah, and Ibn 'Umar. This view is also supported by Malik, ash-Shaf'i, Ahmad, and Ishaq. Another group, including Sufyan and Ibn al-Mubarak, hold that: '*Zakah* should not be taken out of an orphan's property.'"

The Insolvent Debtor

Whoever has property must pay its proper *zakah*. If the property is indebted, he may first pay off his debt, then in case the remainder is enough to constitute a *nisab*, he must pay *zakah*. If he does not hold the *nisab*, he does not have to pay it since he is poor. The Messenger of Allah, upon whom be peace, said: "Only the wealthy are required to give charity." This *hadith* is related by Ahmad and al-Bukhari. The latter records it in *mu'allaq* form. The Prophet also said: "*Zakah* is levied on the rich and paid to the poor." It is all the same, whether he is indebted to Allah or to man, because one *hadith* states: "Allah's debt is more deserving of fulfillment."

Zakah Owed by a Deceased Person

If a person dies before he pays *zakah*, then it must be taken from his estate.

According to ash-Shaf'i, Ahmad, Ishaq, and Abu Thaur, it is obligatory that *zakah* be paid from the property of the deceased, and this payment receives preference over debt, legacy, and inheritance for Allah says: "... after payment of legacies and debts is what you leave ..." [*an-Nisa'*: 12]. *Zakah* is a debt payable to Allah.

A man came to the Messenger of Allah, upon whom be peace, and said: "My mother died while she still had to make up one month of fasting. Shall I make it up for her?" The Prophet replied: "If there was any debt upon your mother, would you pay it off for her?" The man answered: "Yes." The Prophet then observed: "A debt to Allah is more deserving to be paid off." This is related by al-Bukhari and Muslim.

The *Niyyah* (Intention)

Since the payment of *zakah* is an act of worship, its validity depends upon the expression of one's intention. That is, the *zakah* payer should pay it for the sake of Allah; he should make up his mind, with all of his heart, that *zakah* is an obligation to be discharged. Allah says: "And they are commanded no more than this: to worship Allah, sincere in their faith in Him alone" [*al-Bayyinah*: 5].

It is related in al-Bukhari and Muslim that the Prophet, upon whom be peace, said: "The value of [one's] deeds is determined by [one's] intentions; and thus for each shall be according to his intentions." Malik and ash-Shaf'i say that the intention is to be made at the time of rendering *zakah*. Abu Hanifah holds that the intention must be present at the time of payment or when *zakah* is being set aside from one's assets. Ahmad's view is that it is permissible to express the *niyyah* a little earlier before payment.

Payment of *Zakah* in Due Time

Zakah must be paid immediately at its due time. Deferring payment of *zakah* is prohibited, unless the payer for some valid reason cannot pay it on time. In such a case, he may wait until he is able to pay it. It is related by Ahmad and al-Bukhari that 'Uqbah ibn al-Harith said: "Once I performed the *'asr* prayer with the Prophet, upon whom be peace. When he concluded the prayer, he hurriedly went to his house and returned immediately. Noticing the amazed faces, he said: 'I left at home a piece of gold which was meant for *sadaqah*, and I did not want to let it remain a night in my house, so I ordered it to be distributed.'"

Ash-Shaf'i and al-Bukhari (the latter in his *Tarikh*) relate from 'Aishah that the Prophet, upon whom be peace, said: "Whenever *sadaqah* which is payable is mixed with a property, it will destroy that property." The same *hadith* is related by al-Humaydi with this addition: "If you have to pay *sadaqah* which is payable, then it must be set aside, or the unlawful [property] will destroy the lawful one."

Paying *Zakah* in Advance

It is permissible for *zakah* to be paid for even two years in advance. Az-Zuhri did not see any problem in paying his *zakah* before the *hawl*. Al-Hasan was once asked if a man who had paid his *zakah* for three years in advance fulfilled his obligation. Al-Hasan answered in the affirmative. Of this view, ash-Shaukani said: "This was the view of ash-Shaf'i, Ahmad, and Abu Hanifah. It was supported by al-Hadi and al-Qasim." Al-Mu'ayyad-billah also subscribes to this opinion as being better, but he says that Malik, Rabi'ah, Sufyan ath-Thauri, Dawud, Abu 'Ubayd ibn al-Harith, and an-Nasir (who comes from the Prophet's family) held that one's obligation is not discharged if the *zakah* is paid before the expiration of the year. They formulated their stance on the Prophet's *hadith*, already mentioned, which makes the *zakah* mandatory for the payer only when he has his possessions for a year. However, this does not invalidate the view of those who maintain that paying *zakah* in advance is lawful, for undeniably the obligation of *zakah* is associated with the expiry of one full year. The difference is only on the point of whether one's obligation is discharged if the *zakah* is paid before the year has expired." Ibn Rushd sums up the subject: "The controversy arises from the question whether it is an act of worship or an obligation owed to the poor. The group which considers it an act of worship, like *salah* (prayers), does not agree that it should be paid before its time. On the other hand, the group which views it as similar to the case of deferred obligatory dues approves its voluntary payment in advance." In support of his view, ash-Shaf'i relates a *hadith* from 'Ali that the Prophet, upon whom be peace, asked for al-'Abbas's *sadaqah* before its due date.

Invoking Blessing for the *Zakah* Payer

It is desirable that the recipient invoke blessing for the *zakah* payer at the time of its payment, for Allah says: "Take alms of their property that you may purify and sanctify them and pray for them. Verily, your prayers are a comfort for them" [*at-Taubah*: 103]. It is related from 'Abdullah ibn Abu Awfa that the Messenger of Allah, upon whom be peace, on receiving *sadaqah* would say: "O Allah, bless the family of Abu Aufa." This is related by Ahmad and others.

Wa'il ibn Hajr reported that the Prophet, upon whom be peace, prayed for a man who had offered a fine she-camel in his *zakah* payment: "May Allah bless him and make his camels beneficial to him." This is related by an-Nasa'i.

Ash-Shaf'i says: "According to this *hadith*, the leader may pray for the almsgiver upon receiving his payment by saying: 'May Allah reward you in turn of what you have offered, and may Allah bless what you still possess.' "*

---

*Supplications:

اللهم صلِّ على آل أبي أوفى
اللهم بارك فيه وفي إبله
آجرك اللَّه فيما أعطيت ، وبارك لك فيما أبقيْت

HOLDINGS SUBJECT TO *ZAKAH*

Islam enjoined *zakah* on crops, fruit, livestock, merchandise, minerals, gold, silver, and treasures.

Zakah on Gold and Silver: Its Obligation

Says Allah concerning *zakah* on gold and silver: "... As for those who hoard treasures of gold and silver and do not spend them for the sake of Allah — warn them of grievous suffering [in the life to come]" [*at-Taubah*: 34]. Thus, *zakah* is prescribed for gold and silver — whether they are in the form of coins, ingots, or dust — as long as the amount owned constitutes a *nisab*, a period of a year has passed, debts are settled, and/or basic needs satisfied from it.

The *Nisab* of Gold and Its Due

The minimum of *nisab* for gold is twenty *dinars* owned for one year. Its due is a quarter of a tenth, that is, half a *dinar*. For any amount over twenty *dinars*, a quarter of a tenth is levied upon it. 'Ali reported that the Prophet, upon whom be peace, said: "There is nothing upon you in gold, until it reaches twenty *dinars*. Thus, if you have twenty *dinars* at the end of the year, then there is half a *dinar* levied on it [as *zakah*]. Any additional amount will be calculated in this manner. There is no *zakah* on property until it has been owned for one year." This *hadith* is related by Ahamd, Abu Dawud, and al-Baihaqi. Al-Bukhari grades it authentic and al-Hafidh verified it.

Zuraiq, the Fazarah clan's protege, reported that 'Umar ibn 'Abdulaziz wrote to him after he became caliph: "Take what passes by you of the commerce of the Muslims — those who trade with their properties — a *dinar* for each forty *dinars*. From that which is less than forty, calculate on the lesser amount until it reaches twenty *dinars*. If you have to take one-third of a *dinar*, disregard it and do not take anything on it. Afterwards, give them a written release of what you have levied from them until the year expires." This is related by Ibn Abu Shaibah.

Malik says in his *al-Muwatta'*: "The uncontroversial tradition that we have is that the *zakah* due on twenty *dinars* is like the *zakah* due on two hundred *dirhams*." Twenty *dinars* are equal to twenty-eight Egyptian *dirhams* in weight.

The *Nisab* of Silver and its Due

There is no *zakah* on silver until the amount exceeds two hundred *dirhams*. The amount payable is a quarter of a tenth for any amount. There is no *zakah* exemption on (silver) coins if they attain a *nisab*.

'Ali reported that the Prophet, upon whom be peace, said: "I exempt you from paying *zakah* on horses and slaves. Pay, then, *zakah* on silver, one *dirham* for each forty *dirhams*. *Zakah* is not due on ninety or one hundred *dirhams* of silver. If it reaches two hundred *dirhams*, five *dirhams* are to be paid." This was related by the authors of *as-Sunnan* (The Traditions). At-Tirmidhi relates: "I asked al-Bukhari if he confirms this *hadith*. He said: 'It is authentic.'" At-Tirmidhi also says: "Jurists recognize that *sadaqah* should be taken out of any amount less than five ounces (*awaq*). One ounce (*uqiyyah*) equals forty *dirhams*. Five *awaq equal 200 dirhams*. Two hundred *dirhams* equal twenty-seven *riyals* equal 555 1/2 Egyptian *piasters*."

Combining Gold and Silver

If a person owns gold and silver, but neither of them on its own constitutes a *nisab*, he should not combine the two in order to obtain a *nisab*. This is because they are not of the same kind. The basic rule is that no category can be combined with another. It is the same for cows and sheep. For example, if someone has 199 *dirhams* and nineteen *dinars*, he is not supposed to pay *zakah* on them.

Zakah on Debt

Debts are of two kinds: (1) A debt which is acknowledged by the debtor with the willingness to pay it off, and (2) A debt which is not acknowledged either because the borrower is insolvent or its payment is deferred.

In the first case, scholars have formed the following views:

The first view: 'Ali, ath-Thauri, Abu Thaur, the Hanafiyyah, and the Hanbaliyyah hold that the creditor should pay *zakah* on the debt, provided he has received it from the debtor, in that *zakah* will be payable retroactively.

The second view: 'Uthman, Ibn 'Umar, Jabir, Tawus, an-Nakha'i, al-Hasan, az-Zuhri, Qatadah, and ash-Shaf'i hold that the creditor should pay *zakah* on the value of a debt owed on time, even though he did not receive it yet, since he is eventually going to receive it and use it. It is similar to the *zakah* of any deposited amount.

The third view: 'Ikrimah, 'Aishah, and Ibn 'Umar hold that no *zakah* is due on debt since it does not grow. It is similar to the case of acquired assets.

The fourth view: Sa'id ibn al-Musayyab and 'Ata ibn Abu Rabah hold that *zakah* should be paid for one year if the debt is returned to the creditors.

(2) For the second case, Qatadah, Ishaq ibn Abu Thaur, and the Hanifiyyah hold that its *zakah* is not compulsory on this type of debt, since the creditor cannot benefit from it. Ath-Thauri and Abu 'Ubayd hold that on receipt (of it) the creditor should pay its *zakah* retroactively since it his and he may use it at his own free will, like the *zakah* on the debt of a rich person. The last two views are attributed to ash-Shaf'i. 'Umar ibn 'Abdulaziz, al-Hasan, al-Layth, al-Auza'i and Malik agree that he should pay *zakah* on it for only one year when he receives it.

Zakah on Banknotes and Bonds

Since they are documents with guaranteed credits, banknotes and bonds are subject to *zakah* once they attain the minimum of *nisab* — that is, a person may change them into currency immediately. The minimum of *nisab* is twenty-seven Egyptian *riyals*.

Zakah on Jewelry

Scholars agree that no *zakah* has to be paid on diamonds, pearls, sapphires, rubies, corals, chrysolite, or any kind of precious stones unless they are used for trade. There is, however, disagreement over whether women's gold or silver jewelry is exempt. Abu Hanifah and Ibn Hazm hold that *zakah* is compulsory on gold and silver jewelry provided they constitute a *nisab*. Their view is based on the report of 'Amr ibn Shu'aib from his father from his grandfather: "Two women with gold bracelets on their wrists came to the Prophet, upon whom be peace. The Prophet said: 'Do you want Allah to make you wear bracelets of fire on the Day of Judgment?' They answered: 'No.' He said: 'Then pay the *zakah* which is due on what you wear on your wrists.' "

In the same way, Asma' bint Yazid reported: "My aunt and I, while wearing gold bracelets, went to the Prophet, upon whom be peace. He asked: 'Did you pay their *zakah*?' She related that they had not. The Prophet said: 'Do you not fear that Allah will make you wear a bracelet of fire? Pay its *zakah*.' " Al-Haythami confirms that it was narrated by Ahmad, and its chain is good.

'Aishah narrated: "The Messenger of Allah, upon whom be peace, came to me and saw me wearing silver rings. Thereupon, he asked: 'What is this, 'Aishah?' I replied: 'I made them to adorn myself for you, O Messenger of Allah.' He said: 'Did you pay their *zakah*?' I said: 'No, or what Allah wishes.' Then he said: 'Their punishment in Hell is enough for you.' " This is related by Abu Dawud, ad-Daraqutni, and al-Baihaqi.

Malik, ash-Shaf'i, and Ahmad ibn Hanbal hold that there is no *zakah* on women's jewelry regardless of its value. Al-Baihaqi relates that Jabir ibn 'Abdullah was once asked if jewelry was subject to *zakah*. He replied that it was not, even if its value exceeded one thousand *dinars*.

Al-Baihaqi also narrates the case of Asma': "Asma' bint Abu Bakr used to adorn her daughters with gold. Although its value was around fifty thousand *dinars*, she did not pay *zakah* on it."

It is related in *al-Muwatta'* from 'Abdurrahman ibn al-Qasim from his father that 'Aishah used to take care of her nieces, who were orphans under her protection, and adorned them with jewelry without paying its *zakah*. Also in *al-Muwatta'* it is related that 'Abdullah ibn 'Umar used to adorn his daughters and slave girls with gold without paying *zakah*.

Summing up the subject, al-Khattabi concludes: "What appears in the Qur'an supports the view of those who hold that *zakah* is obligatory on gold and silver, and the traditions also support this. Those who did not consider it obligatory based their view on speculation and some of the traditions. However, to be on the safe side, it is better to pay." These different views deal with allowable gold or silver adornment. As for other adornments which are prohibited – that is, a woman wearing a man's adornment – their *zakah* should be paid. The same rule is applied to gold or silver utensils.

Zakah on a Woman's Dowry

Abu Hanifah is of the opinion that there is no *zakah* on the dowry of a woman until she comes to possess it. At the same time, the dowry must constitute the *nisab* at the end of the year. The position, however, will be different if the woman has accumulated a *nisab* other than the dowry. In such a case, any amount she receives should be added to the *nisab*, and *zakah* should be paid at the end of a year of possession. Ash-Shaf'i holds that a woman must pay *zakah* on her dowry at the end of one year, even if it is before the wedding. The probability of its restitution because of nullification, or its fifty percent refund because of divorce, does not exempt her from paying it. The Hanbaliyyah are of the opinion that dowry is a credit for women and that it is similar to debts. If the recipient of a dowry is rich, the payment of its *zakah* is obligatory. If the recipient is insolvent, or does not acknowledge it, then, according to al-Khiraqiyy, the *zakah* is obligatory regardless of the consumation of marriage. If a woman receives half of her dowry (in the case of her divorce before consumation), she should pay *zakah* only on the received half. However, if all of the dowry is cancelled before she receives it (in the case of nullifying the marriage on her behalf), she is under no obligation to pay its *zakah*.

Zakah on House Rent

Abu Hanifah and Malik maintain that the rent is not payable to the landlord at the time of the contract but at the expiry of the renting period. Thus, the landlord who rents out a house should pay the *zakah* on his house rent, provided the fixed amount meets the following conditions: receiving of the money and completion of *nisab* at the end of the year. The Hanbaliyyah think that once the contract is concluded, the landlord is entitled to have rent. Thus, if someone leases his house, the *zakah* is due upon its fixed rate reaching a *nisab* at the end of the year. This is so because the landlord has the right to spend the rent the way he wants to. The possibility of cancelling the lease does not invalidate the obligation to pay *zakah*. This case is similar to the case of dowry before the consumation of a marriage. If the rent is an arrear rent, then it should be treated as a debt either as paid or postponed. In *al-Majmu'*, an-Nawawi says: "If somebody leased a house and was paid in advance, he should pay its *zakah* on receiving it. This is uncontroversial."

Zakah on Trade

The majority of scholars among the companions, the followers, the generation after them, and the jurists who came subsequently held that *zakah* on merchandise is compulsory. Abu Dawud and al-Baihaqi relate that Samurah ibn Jundub reported: "The Prophet, upon whom be peace, used to command us to pay *sadaqah* from [the goods] we had for sale." Ad-Daraqutni and al-Baihaqi relate that Abu Dharr reported the Prophet, upon whom be peace, saying: "There is *sadaqah* on camels, sheep, cows, and house furniture." Ash-Shaf'i, Ahmad, Abu 'Ubaid, ad-Daraqutni, al-Baihaqi, and 'Abd ur-Razzaq relate that Abu 'Amr ibn Hammas reported from his father that he said: "I used to sell leather and containers. Once, 'Umar ibn al-Khattab passed by me and said: 'Pay the *sadaqah* due on your property.' I said: 'O Commander of the Faithful, it is just leather.' He replied: 'Evaluate it and then pay its due *sadaqah.'*"

Commenting on its credentials, Ibn Quadmah says in *al-Mughni* that this is a kind of story which is well-known and indisputable. This might be a consensus of opinion.

On the other hand, the Zahiriyyah maintain that merchandise is not subject to *zakah*. They differ, says Ibn Rushd, because of their use of analogical reasoning to the obligation of *zakah* and because of their disagreement on the authenticity of Samurah's and Abu Dharr's reports.

However, the majority of jurists view merchandise as a property which increases in value. Hence, by analogy, it is similar to the three categories upon which *zakah* must be paid: plantations, cattle, and gold and silver.

It is stated in *al-Manār*: "Most scholars agree that *zakah* is obligatory on merchandise even though there is no clear-cut ruling in the Qur'an or the *sunnah* on this issue. However, there are a number of reports that corroborate each other with regard to the evidence provided by [their] texts. Their rationale is that since merchandise is a form of cash, there is no difference between it and *dinars* or *dirhams* in terms of which it is valued. This means that the form of the *nisab* can alternate between value in the form of cash and that which is valued in the form of merchandise. If *zakah* had not been obligatory on merchandise, the rich — or most of them — would have converted their cash into merchandise for trading purposes, making sure that the *nisab* of gold and silver is never possessed by them for a year."

The main consideration here is that by levying *zakah* on the rich, Allah the Exalted wants to help the poor and to promote the welfare of the people in general. For the rich, its benefit lies in cleansing their persons of stinginess — both in money and feelings. For the poor, its benefit lies in easing their circumstances. *Zakah* thus eliminates the causes of corruption which results from the increase of money in a few hands. It is this wisdom which the Qur'an refers to when it deals with the distribution of booty: "... that it becomes not a commodity between the rich among you" (*al-Hashr*: 7). Therefore, it is not reasonable to exempt businessmen from their societal obligations when they possess most of the nation's wealth.

When Goods can be Judged as Trading Goods

The author of *al-Mughnī* states that: "Merchandise can only be considered as trading goods for two reasons: (1) The actual possession of merchandise is acquired by an act such as a commercial transaction, marriage, divorce demanded by the wife (*khul'*), acceptance of a gift, bequest, booty, and other lawful acquisition. This is because that which is not subject to *zakah* cannot be considered as so subsequent to its possession on the basis of *niyyah* (intention) only, as, for example, in the case of fasting. It does not make any difference whether a person came to possess such items by buying them or not because his possession is by an act similar to inheritance. (2) The goods are intended, at the time of possession, for trade. These are considered as non-trade goods even though the person intends to use them later for trade.

However, if he possesses these goods through inheritance and intends them for trade, they are not considered as trade goods because the determining factor in such cases is the status of acquisition, not the temporary state of trade. Mere intention will not provide a valid reason to change its status. For example, if a person intends to travel without embarking upon it, then the mere expression of his intention will not constitute the act of traveling. Likewise, if a person bought merchandise for trade and then intended it for possession, it would be considered as such and *zakah* will not be paid on it.

How is *Zakah* on Trade Money to be Paid?

One who possesses merchandise with a *nisab* for a year should pay *zakah* on it, the amount of which is a quarter of a tenth of its value. This should be done by a businessman every year. However, the period of a year does not come into effect unless his inventory constitutes a *nisab*.

Assuming a businessman possesses merchandise short of a *nisab* and part of a year has passed, his inventory subsequently increases through an unusual rise in value (because of supply and demand or through price fluctuation) so that it constitutes a *nisab*; or he sold merchandise for the price of a *nisab*; or during the course of the year he comes to possess other merchandise which, together with his previous amount, completes a *nisab*; then, the *hawl* (for the purpose of *zakah*) starts at that time, and the time elapsed is not taken into consideration. This is the view of the Hanafiyyah, ath-Thauri, ash-Shaf'i, Ishaq, Abu 'Ubaid, Abu Thaur, and Ibn al-Mundhir.

According to Abu Hanifah, if the merchandise in possession constitutes a *nisab* at the beginning of the year and also at the end, *zakah* will still be applicable even though the *nisab* might have decreased within that time. The reason is that it is difficult to ascertain its completeness in the intervening period.

The Hanbaliyyah hold that if the merchandise decreases during the course of the year and increases again until it constitutes a *nisab*, the (requisite) period of a year starts all over again because it has been interrupted in its course by the decrease.

ZAKAH ON PLANTS AND FRUIT

Allah has made *zakah* obligatory on plants and fruit, for He says: "O you who believe! Spend of the good things which you have earned, and of that which We bring forth from the earth" [*al-Baqarah*: 267]. *Zakah* is called expenditure (*nafaqah*). Giving the justification for paying *zakah* on produce, Allah says: "He it is who produces gardens trellised and untrellised, and the date palm and the crops of diverse flavors, and the olive, and the pomegranate, like and unlike. Eat of the fruit thereof when it produces fruit, and pay its due upon the harvest day" [*al-An'am*: 141]. In his explanation of the word *haqq* (due) in the preceding *'ayah*, Ibn 'Abbas says that by *haqq* is meant both the obligatory *zakah* and the *'ushr* (tithe) and the half-tithe.

Zakah on Plants and Fruits at the Time of the Prophet

During the time of the Prophet, upon whom be peace, *zakah* was levied on wheat, barley, dates, and raisins.

Abu Burdah related from Abu Musa and Mu'adh that when the Messenger of Allah, upon whom be peace, sent the (latter two) to Yemen to teach its inhabitants Islam, he commanded them to levy *sadaqah* only on wheat, barley, dates, and raisins. This *hadith* is related by ad-Daraqutni, al-Hakim, at-Tabarani, and al-Baihaqi.

Commenting on the status of the report, al-Baihaqi says that its chain is *muttasil* (uninterrupted) and its narrators are credible.

Whether *sadaqah* on such items should be considered *zakah* or not, Ibn al-Mundhir and ibn 'Abd al-Barr say: "The scholars are of the opinion that *sadaqah* is obligatory on wheat, barley, dates, and raisins." This opinion has its roots in a saying by Ibn Majah that the Messenger, upon whom be peace, regulated the payment of *zakah* on wheat, barley, dates, raisins and corn. Muhammad ibn 'Ubaidullah al-'Arzumi, a narrator in its chain, however, is of questionable status in the eyes of the scholars, and as such, his report is not credible.

Plants and Fruits Which Were Not Subject to *Zakah*

Zakah was not levied on vegetables or fruit, with the exception of grapes and fresh dates (*rutab*). 'Ata ibn as-Sa'ib reported that 'Abdullah ibn al-Mughirah wanted to levy *sadaqah* on Musa ibn Talha's vegetables. The latter objected, saying: "You have no right to do that. The Messenger of Allah used to say: 'There is no *sadaqah* on this [vegetables].' " This is related by ad-Daraqutni, al-Hakim, and al-Athram in his *Sunan*. This *hadith* is *mursal*.

Musa ibn Talhah says: "Five things [which were subject to *zakah*] were mentioned by the Messenger of Allah, upon whom be peace: barley, wheat, *sult* [a kind of barley having no husk], raisins, and dates. Whatever else the land produces is not subject to the *'ushr*. It is also reported that Mu'adh did not levy *sadaqah* on vegetables."

Commenting on the status of these reports, al-Baihaqi says: "All of these *ahadith* are of the *mursal* kind but were reported from different authorities. Nevertheless, they confirm each other." The *hadith* on this subject include the sayings of 'Umar, 'Ali, and 'Aishah.

Al-Athram narrated that one of Caliph 'Umar's governors wrote to him concerning grape plantations, including peaches and pomegranates which produced twice as much harvest as the grapes. He wrote back: "There is no *'ushr* (tithe) on them. They pertain to *'udah* — items that cannot be distributed in inheritance."

At-Tirmidhi agrees with the preceding and says: "The practice [based upon this] among most jurists is not to levy *sadaqah* on vegetables." Al-Qurtubi also supports this: "*Zakah* is to be levied on the *muqtat* [land products used as stable food] and not on vegetables." In at-Ta'if, they used to grow pomegranates, peaches, and

citrus, but there is no confirmation that the Prophet and his succes-
sors levied *zakah* on them.

Ibn al-Qayyim contends: "It was not his [the Prophet's] practice to levy *zakah* on horses, slaves, mules, donkeys, and vegetables,
melons, cucumbers, and fruits, which cannot be stored or measured
by capacity. The only exceptions were grapes and fresh dates. On
the latter two kinds, *zakah* was levied as a whole, without differen-
tiation whether or not they were dry."

The Opinion of Jurists

There is no difference of opinion among jurists concerning
the obligatory nature of *zakah* on plants and fruits. They do,
however, differ on the kinds of plants and fruits which should be
subject to *zakah*. Here is the broad spectrum of opinions on the
subject:

Al-Hasan al-Basri and ash-Shu'abi hold that *zakah* is only on
the specified items (in the Qur'an and *sunnah*) — that is corn, dates,
and raisins — since other kinds are not mentioned. Ash-Shaukani
upholds this view.

Abu Hanifah maintains that *zakah* is due on every type of
produce of the land including vegetables, but excluding what is not
intentionally planted and cultivated such as firewood, bamboo,
grass, and those trees which bear no fruit. His opinion is based upon
the general meaning of the Prophet's saying: "From what the heavens irrigate, a tithe [is due]." The meaning is general and encompasses all types of arable products, which are planted to make the
land grow, and therefore refers to any agricultural practices similar
to the growing of grains (*habb*).

Abu Yusuf and Muhammad hold that *zakah* is payable on
every product of the land, provided it lasts the whole year without
too much care or treatment. This includes produce measured by
capacity, such as grains, or by mass, such as cotton and sugar. If the
produce does not last a whole year, such as the two kinds of cucumber (*quththa'* and *khiyar*), watermelons and others of their kind,
there is no *zakah* on them.

Malik holds that *zakah* is payable on that which is produced
on the land and which stays, becomes dry, and is planted by human
beings. This includes land produce used as nonperishable food
(*muqtat*), such as safflower and sesame seeds. According to him,
there is no *zakah* on vegetables and fruits such as figs,
pomegranates and apples. Ash-Shaf'i maintains that *zakah* is pay-

able on any produce, provided the resulting crop is used as regular food which can be stored and planted by human beings, such as grains and barley.

An-Nawawi says: "Our opinion is that there is no *zakah* on any trees other than palm and grapevines. There is also no *zakah* on grains other than the one which is or can be stored, and no *zakah* on vegetables." Ahmad is of the opinion that there is *zakah* on everything that Allah causes the land to produce, such as grains and fruits, that can be dried, preserved, measured and planted by human beings, whether they be considered nonperishable foods, such as wheat and *qutniyyat* (including peas, beans, lentils and such other grains), or spices and herbs (*abariz*), such as coriander, caraway seeds, or seeds such as linseed of the fluz plant (*kittan* seeds), the seeds of the two kinds of cucumber (*quth-tha'* and *khiyar*), or safflower and sesame seeds.

According to Ahmad, *zakah* is also payable on dry fruits such as dates, raisins, apricots, figs, almonds, hazel nuts, and pistachio nuts if the preceding specifications apply to them. There is no *zakah* on fresh fruit such as peaches, pears, apples, apricots, and figs. In the same way, it is not due on vegetables such as the two kinds of cucumber, watermelons, eggplants, turnips, and carrots.

Zakah on Olives

An-Nawawi says: "As for olives, our [Shaf'iyyah] view is that there is no *zakah* on them." This is also the opinion of Hasan ibn Salih, Ibn Abu Layla, and Abu 'Ubaid.

Scholars such as as-Zuhri, al-Auza'i, al-Layth, Malik, ath-Thauri, Abu Hanifah, and Abu Thaur maintain that there is *zakah* on olives. Az-Zuhri, al-Layth, and al-Auza'i hold: "Determine its quantity by conjecture (*yukharras*), and then take its *zakah* in the form of olive oil," while Malik says: "There is no need to compute its quantity by conjecture (*yukharras*). Take a tithe subsequent to the olives being pressed and attain the weight of five *awsuq*."

The Origin of the Different Opinions Concerning Zakah on Plants and Fruits

Of their differences on the payment of *zakah* pertaining to plants and fruits, Ibn Rushd informs us: "The difference of opinion lies in the fact that some jurists confine paying of *zakah* to only those items of consumption which are generally agreed upon, while others go beyond those items and include dried fruits in them too. [The crux of the issue is]: What qualifies the four edible items [wheat, barley, dates, and dried grapes] for *zakah*? Are they subject to *zakah* because of their being delineated as such or because of their special import to the subsistence of life? Those who subscribe to the first view restrict payment of *zakah* to the four edibles, and those who subscribe to the second view extend the obligation to all land produce except for grass, firewood, and bamboo. There is a consensus on the latter being excluded from *zakah*. However, when it comes to the use of analogy based on a general statement, both groups rest on shaky ground."

The saying of the Prophet, which uses the expression *al-ladhi yaqtadhi*, reads: "From what the heavens water, a tithe [is due], and from what is watered by irrigation [*nadh*] a half a tithe." The relative pronoun *ma* is used to mean *al-ladhi*, which is a general expression. Allah, the Exalted, also says: "It is He who has brought into being gardens — both the cultivated ones and those growing wild — and the date palm, and fields bearing multiform produce, and the olive trees, and the pomegranate: all resembling one another and yet so different. Eat of their fruit when it comes to fruition, and give unto the poor their due on the harvest day . . ." [*al-An'am*: 141].

Analogically speaking, *zakah* aims at counteracting poverty and this cannot be done through *zakah* on land produce which is edible and sustains life.

Restricting a general statement with this kind of analogical reasoning vitiates *zakah* on all land produce except ones which sustain life. Those who follow the general import of the Prophet's saying add some more to the generally acknowledged four items. Excluded of course are the ones on which there is consensus.

Again, those who agree upon land produce of a subsistance kind often differ over whether it can be considered as being subsistent. Can analogical reasoning be the basis of what they agree upon or not? An example of such a disagreement is that of Malik and ash-Shaf'i regarding olives. Malik holds that *zakah* on olives is obligatory, while ash-Shaf'i is against it, according to a latter view expressed in Egypt. The reason for his disagreement is whether olives could be considered as food vital for life or not.

Nisab of Plants and Fruits

Most scholars say that there is no *zakah* on plants or fruits until they attain the amount of five *awsuq*. Furthermore, this becomes applicable only after the chaff, straw, and husk are removed. If it is not cleansed of husk, then the amount of *zakah* would be ten *awsuq*.

Abu Hurairah reported that the Prophet, upon whom be peace, said: "There is no *sadaqah* (*zakah*) on that which is less than five *awsuq*." It is also narrated by Ahmad and al-Baihaqi with a good chain.

Abu Sa'id al-Khudri reported that the Prophet, upon whom be peace, said: "There is no *sadaqah* on any amount of dates or grains less than five *awsuq*." A *wusuq* by consensus of opinion is sixty *sa'as* (a cubic measure of varying magnitude). This *hadith* is said to be *munqati* that is — a *hadith* with an interrupted chain.

Both Abu Hanifah and Mujahid hold that *zakah* is due on any amount, little or big, in accordance with the generic nature of the Prophet's saying: "From what the heavens water, a tithe [is due] ..." This is because land produce is perishable and cannot be preserved for a whole year. In that case, such produce does not attain a *nisab* within a one-year period.

Ibn al-Qayyim's discussion of the subject is that the authentic and explicit *sunnah* for a tithe's *nisab* is the *hadith*: "From what the heavens water, a tithe [is due], and from what is watered by irrigation (*gharb* - vessel) a half a tithe." This is applicable to both small and large quantities as opposed to the specific amount mentioned in other *ahadith*. In its application, a generic statement is as important as a specific one. Should there be a conflict between the two, then the most comprehensive will be applicable. This is the rule.

It has been said that both of the preceding *ahadith* ought to be followed. In their essence, they do not contradict each other, nor does one of them have to cancel the other. The Messenger of Allah, upon whom be peace, has to be obeyed in this matter, for he said: "From what the heavens water, a tithe [is due] ..." This saying seeks to distinguish between the two (categories): one on which a tithe is due, and the other on which only half of the tithe is due. He therefore distinguished between the two categories only in respect to the amount due. There is no mention of any amount of *nisab* in this *hadith*. However, he mentioned it explicitly in another *hadith* which cannot be ignored as something that is general or is intended to be so and not otherwise. It is similar to other statements of general import which have been explained in the texts.

Ibn Qudamah concludes: "The saying of the Prophet, upon whom be peace, that 'there is no *sadaqah* [*zakah*] on anything less than five *awsuq*' is agreed upon. This *hadith* is specific, and for this reason takes precedence and clarifies his previous statement of general import. This is similar to his saying that '*zakah* is due on all freely grazing camels,' which becomes explicit by his other saying on the same subject: 'There is no *sadaqah* on less than five camels.' Likewise his saying: '*Sadaqah* on silver is a fourth of the tithe,' becomes specific by a latter utterance: 'There is no *sadaqah* on any amount less than five ounces.' Thus, it is possible to have holdings which qualify for *sadaqah* per se, but on which it is not levied."

When it comes to land produce, possession of a property for a year cannot be used as criterion, because their maturity or growth is completed by the time of harvest, and not by their continuity extended beyond a year. However, possession is considered for goods other than land produce since it is generally assumed that by the end of the year they must have completed their growth. The principle of attaining a *nisab* on any property is based on the understanding that a *nisab* is an amount large enough to be subjected to *zakah*. This may be explained by recalling that *sadaqah* is obligatory for the rich, which presupposes the existence of *nisab* generated by their holdings. For produce which cannot be measured but qualifies for *zakah*, a *sa'a* is used. One *sa'a* is a measure equal to one and one-third cups (*qadah*). Thus, a *nisab* is fifty *kaylah*.[1] As to the produce which cannot be measured, Ibn Quadamah says: "The *nisab* of saffron, cotton and such items is to be weighed at 1,600 Iraqi pounds (*ratl*).[2] Thus, its weight is estimated."

Abu Yusuf says that if the produce cannot be measured, then *zakah* can only be levied on it when its value attains the *nisab* of articles subject to the lowest standard of measurement. Thus, *zakah* will not be levied on cotton until its value reaches

---

[1]*Kaylah*: a dry measure of weight. In Egypt it is equal to 16.72 L.

[2]Five *awsuq* equal 1,600 Iraqi *ratl*. An Iraqi *ratl* equals approximately 130 *dirhams*.

five *awsuq* of an article to the lowest value so measured, such as barley and the like. This is because it is impossible to measure the article in itself except by the lower price of two *nisabs*. According to Muhammad ibn al-Hasan: "For *zakah*, a product has to reach five times the greatest value of its kind. Thus, *zakah* is not payable on cotton when it reaches five *qintars*,[3] because evaluation by means of *wusuq* is based on the consideration that its value is higher than what is valued in kind."

The Rate of *Zakah*

The rate of *zakah* differs according to the method of irrigation. If it is watered naturally without the use of artificial means, then the *zakah* payable is a tithe (one-tenth) of the produce. However, if it is irrigated by a mechanical device or with purchased water, then the *zakah* payable is half a tithe.

Mu'adh reports that the Prophet, upon whom be peace, said: "On that which is watered by the heavens, or by an adjacent water channel, a tithe is due. As for what is irrigated through a well or a stream, its *zakah* is half a tithe." This *hadith* is narrated by al-Baihaqi and al-Hakim, and is graded *sahih*.

Ibn 'Umar reported that the Prophet, upon whom be peace, said: "On that which is watered by the heavens or springs or its own roots, a tithe is due, and on that watered by a well or a stream, half a tithe." This *hadith* is narrated by al-Bukhari and others.

In case the land is watered equally by artificial as well as natural means, then *zakah* payable will be three-fourths of a tithe.

Ibn Qudamah stated that he did not know of any difference of opinion on the preceding *hadith*. If one method of watering is used more than the other, then for calculating *zakah*, this would be the determining factor. This is the view of Abu Hanifah, Ahmad, ath-Thauri, and ash-Shaf'i (one of his two opinions).

All of the costs involved in harvesting, transportation, threshing, cleaning, storing, and others are to be borne by the owner from his property and should not be accounted for against the *zakah* to be paid.

Ibn 'Abbas and Ibn 'Umar hold that whatever is borrowed for the purpose of tilling, planting, and harvesting should first be taken out.

---

[3] A varying weight of 100 pounds. In Egypt it is equal to 44.93 kg.

This is evident from their following statements reported by Jabir ibn Zaid that Ibn 'Abbas and Ibn 'Umar said that a man who borrows in order to spend it either on cultivation (of his land) or on his family must first pay off his debt, then pay *zakah* on the rest. Ibn 'Abbas said: "First he must pay off what he spent on cultivation, and then pay *zakah* on the rest." Yahya ibn Adam related this in *al-Kharaj*.

Ibn Hazm relates from 'Ata that all expenses are to be deducted first. If *zakah* is applicable to the remaining amount, only then will it be paid.

Zakah on *Kharajiyyah* Land

Land subject to tax is divided into two categores: (1) *'ushriyyah* land (tithe land): land owned by people who accepted Islam willingly or who were conquered by force and had their land divided among the conquerors, or land revived and cultivated by Muslims; and (2) *kharajiyyah* land (taxable land), land conquered by force and left to its original owners on the condition that they pay the required land tax.

Just as *zakah* is payable on *'ushriyyah*, so it is paid on *kharajiyyah* when the inhabitants of the latter accept Islam or when a Muslim buys it. In that case, both the tithe and the *kharaj* become due, and neither of them will negate the application of the other.

Ibn al-Mundhir witnesses: "This is the view of most of the scholars, including 'Umar ibn 'Abdulaziz, Rabi'ah, az-Zuhri, Yahya al-Ansari, Malik, al-Awzai, ath-Thauri, al-Hasan ibn Salih, Ibn Abu Layla, al-Layth, Ibn al-Mubarak, Ahmad, Ishaq, Abu 'Ubaid, and Dawud." Their opinion is derived from the Qur'an, the *sunnah*, and the exercise of their intellect — that is, by means of analogical reasoning or *qiyas*.

The Qur'anic verse referred to is: "O you who believe! Spend of the good things which you have earned and of that which We produce from the earth for you" [*al-Baqarah*: 267]. Sharing the produce of one's land with the poor is obligatory, whether the land is *kharajiyyah* or *'ushriyyah*. The *sunnah* referred to is: "From what the heavens water, a tithe [is due]." This *hadith* encompasses in its general meaning both the *kharaj* and the *'ushriyyah* land.

As to the analogical reasoning (*qiyas*), both *zakah* and *kharaj* are a kind of obligations (*haqq*), each based on a different reason, and one does not nullify the other. It is similar to the case when a person who is in the state of *ihram*[4] kills privately owned game (for eating). Since the tithe is payable by the force of the text, it cannot be negated by *kharaj*, which becomes payable by the force of *ijtihad*.[5] Abu Hanifah holds that there is no tithe on *kharaj* land. *Kharaj*, he says, is due only when the land is conquered, (whereas) one of the conditions governing the obligatory nature of the tithe is that the land should not be *kharajiyyah*.

The Validity of Abu Hanifah's View

Imam Abu Hanifah provides the following evidence for his view: According to Ibn Mas'ud, the Prophet, upon whom be peace, said: "Neither *kharaj* nor tithe ['*ushr*] are payable simultaneously on the land of a Muslim."

The preceding *hadith* is by consensus held to be weak (*da'if*). Yahya ibn 'Anbasah reported it on the authority of Abu Hanifah from Hammad from Ibrahim an-Nakha'i from 'Alqamah, from Ibn Mas'ud from the Prophet, upon whom be peace.

Al-Baihaqi probes its chain and says in *al-Ma'rifah as-Sunan wa al-Athar*: "The preceding *hadith* is narrated by Abu Hanifah from Hammad from Ibrahim on his own authority. Thus, Yahya reported in suspended (*marfu'*) form." Yahya ibn 'Anbasah is well-known for interpolating unauthentic sayings and attributing them to established authorities. This was related by Abu Ahmad ibn 'Adiyy al-Hafiz as we were informed by Abu Sa'id al-Malini about him."

Likewise, al-Kamal Ibn al-Humam, a leading Hanafiyyah, considers the *hadith* weak.

Ahmad, Muslim, and Abu Dawud relate from Abu Hurairah that the Prophet, upon whom be peace, said: "Iraq would refrain from paying its *qafiz*[6] and *dirham*, Syria its *mudd* and *dinar*, and Egypt its *ardab* and *dinar*. Thus, you would come back from where you had started." He said this three times. Abu Hurairah heard this in person.

---

[4]*Ihram* is the state of ritual consecration during pilgrimage to Makkah. The pilgrim usually wears two seamless white pieces of cloth.

[5]*Ijtihad* is rendered as an independent judgment in a legal or theological question based on the interpretation and application of the four principles of jurisprudence.

[6]*Qafiz, mudd,* and *ardab* are dry measures that were used in these Muslim countries.

This *hadith* does not provide evidence to the effect that *zakah* should not be taken from *kharaj* land. The scholars interpret it to mean that the conversion of these countries to Islam would eliminate land tax. It may also have alluded to dissensions which could prevail at the end of time and which would lead to neglecting or fulfilling the obligation of *zakah, jizyah* and other such dues by them.

An-Nawawi says: "If this *hadith* means what they [the Hanafiyyah] claim, then it means that *zakah* could not be enjoined on *dirhams, dinars*, and merchandise. If this is so, then nobody subscribes to it."

It was reported that when the *dahqan* (grandee) of Bahr al-Mulk embraced Islam, 'Umar ibn al-Khattab said: "Give him the land and collect the land tax from him." This is a clear statement on the matter of taking *kharaj* without demanding payment of the tithe.

This incident indicates that *kharaj* is not cancelled for any person after he embraces Islam, nor does it lead to the cancellation of tithe. He mentioned *kharaj* here as a way of stating that it will not be cancelled by embracing Islam, like *jizyah*. As for the tithe, it is well-known that it is binding on a free Muslim, so there is no need to mention it. He also did not mention the levy of *zakah* on cattle. This holds for the payment of *zakah* on silver and gold and other valuables. Perhaps the *dahqan* (grandee) did not possess anything which required the levy of a tithe on it.

It is said that the practice of the rulers and imams was not to combine the *'ushr* and *kharaj*. Ibn al-Mundhir disapproves of such a practice because 'Umar ibn 'Abdulaziz did combine the two.

It is also said that *kharaj* is the opposite of *'ushr*. This means that *kharaj* is a consequence of conquest, whereas *'ushr* is an act of worship. Therefore, the two cannot be combined (at one time) and obtained simultaneously from the same person. This held true in the beginning (when lands were conquered), but it is not tenable in the long run. Nevertheless, not all forms of *kharaj* are based on force and conquest since some of its forms are instituted without force as, for example, in the case of lands adjoining a *kharaj* land or in the case of acquired and revived land watered with streams.

It is also said that the reason behind the imposition of *kharaj* and *'ushr* is one — that is, an actually or potentially yielding land. This can be explained by recalling that if it is marsh land of no benefit (*sabkhah*), there is no *kharaj* or *'ushr* on it. That is, one cause cannot demand two dues of the same kind. This is similar to the case of an individual who for a year possesses free-grazing camels (*sa'imah*) intended for sale, for such a person is not required to pay two kinds of *zakah* — that is, one for possession and one for trade.

This is not the case because the *'ushr* (tithe) is payable on the land's produce and the *kharaj* on the land itself, regardless of whether it is planted or not. As to the admissibility of the unity of cause, al-Kāmal ibn al-Humam explains there is nothing to prevent two obligations from being connected to one cause, such as land.

Most scholars are of the opinion that anyone who rents a piece of land and cultivates it must pay the *zakah,* not the true owner of that land. To this Abu Hanifah replies: "*Zakah* is due on the land owner." Ibn Rushd holds: "Their difference lies in whether the *'ushr* is payable on the land itself or its produce." Obviously, *zakah,* as their views suggest, is payable on either of them. The difference is only of priority, considering that both the produce and the land belong to the same owner. Most scholars say that *zakah* is due on seeds (*habb*). Abu Hanifah holds that the essence of obligation rests with the land. Ibn Qudamah inclines toward the majority's view and says: "The obligation lies on the produce and is payable by its owner, as in the case of *zakah* on the value [of a property] intended for trade. Also, it is similar to the tithe payable on the produce of the land owned." Their (the Hanafiyyah) view is not authentic, for if *zakah* were to be levied on the value of the land, then it would have been obligatory even if the land was not cultivated, as is the case with the land tax, and even non-Muslims would not be excluded from its application. Be that the case, *kharaj* would have to be estimated on the land itself, not on the value of produce — that is, it would be considered part of the expenditure of fay',[7] not the expenditure of *zakah.*

The Estimation of *Nisab* on Palm Trees and Grapevines Through *Khars*[8], Not by Measure (*Kayl*)

As soon as palm trees and grapevines ripen and their produce is ready to be picked, an estimation of their *nisab* is made without their actual weighing. The process is carried out by a knowledgeable and trustworthy person who estimates the amount of fresh grapes and dates still on the trees for *zakah* as if they were dry dates and raisins. The amount of *zakah* is, however, payable when the fruit becomes dry.

---

[7]*Fay'* are those possessions of unbelievers obtained by Muslims without war.

[8]*Khars* is estimation through conjecture.

Abu Humayd as-Sa'idi related: "We went on the expedition of Tabuk with the Prophet, upon whom be peace. When we arrived at Wadi al-Qura, we saw a woman in her orchard. The Prophet said: 'Let us estimate [her *zakah*].' Then the Messenger, upon whom be peace, estimated ten *awsuq* and told her: '[The amount of *zakah*] has been calculated on your [orchard's] produce.'" This is narrated by al-Bukhari.

This is the practice of the Messenger of Allah, upon whom be peace, and his companions and the scholars observed it.

The Hanafiyyah have different views because they consider conjecture to be uncertain, and therefore, of no use in determining the amount owed. Still, the tradition of the Messenger of Allah is a better guide (*'adha*) because conjecture is not guessing; it is a diligent attempt to estimate the amount of the produce. It is the same as estimating the amount of the produce lost (because of its being rotten or moth-ridden). The basis for conjecture rests on the custom that people eat fresh fruits, and as such, there is no need for calculating the amount of *zakah* before it is eaten or plucked. In this way, the owners are allowed to do what they want and, at the same time, to determine the amount of *zakah*. The appraiser should ignore a third or a fourth of the produce as a reprieve for the property owners since they, their guests, and their neighbors need to eat some of it. Also, the produce is exposed to such perils as birds feeding, passers-by plucking, and wind blowing. Any appraisal of the amount of *zakah* on all of the produce without excluding a third or a fourth of it (for the preceding reasons) would have militated against the genuine interests of the owners.

Sahl ibn Abu Hathamah related that the Prophet, upon whom be peace, said: "Whenever you conjecture, estimate the [*zakah*] and ignore one-third. If you do not, then leave [at least] one-fourth." This is narrated by Ahmad and the authors of *Sunan*, except for Ibn Majah. It was also reported by al-Hakim and Ibn Hibban, and they both authenticated it. Commenting on the status of the report, at-Tirmidhi says: "The *hadith* reported by Sahl is the one enacted or followed by most scholars." Bashir ibn Yassar said: "When 'Umar ibn al-Khattab appointed Abu Hathamah al-Ansari to estimate the property of Muslims, he told him: 'Whenever you see that the people have left some dates unplucked for autumn, leave them for the people to eat, and do not estimate the *zakah* on them.'"

Makhul said: "Whenever the Messenger of Allah, upon whom be peace, assigned someone to estimate, he would say: 'Be easy on the people, for some of their property [trees] could be barren, some low, and some for [their] eating.'" It was narrated by Abu 'Ubaid, who added: "The low palm tree is called *as-sabilah* and allows its fruit to be plucked by passers-by. The eating tree (*al-akilah*) is a palm tree especially designated as an eating tree for the owner's family or for whoever is attached to them."

Eating of the Grains

It is permissible for the owner to eat from the grain, and whatever he consumes will not be included in the quantity subject to *zakah*, for this is a long-standing custom. In any case, only a small amount is actually eaten. It is the same as an owner of a fruit-bearing tree eating some of its produce. Therefore, the *zakah* will be estimated on the actual amount after he harvests the crop and husks the seeds. Ahmad was asked about the eating of *farik* (rubbed green wheat) by the owner, and he answered that there is no harm if the owner eats what he needs. This is also the opinion of ash-Shaf'i, al-Layth and Ibn Hazm. However, Malik and Abu Hanifah hold that the owner will have to account for what he eats.

Combining Grains and Fruit

Scholars agree that various kinds of fruit can be combined even if their quality is different — that is, excellent or bad in quality. Different kinds of raisins may also be combined together, and so can the various kinds of wheat and cereals.

They also agree that merchandise and its cash value received can be combined. Ash-Shaf'i allows combining goods and cash only when purchased because the *nisab* is calculated upon that. Scholars also do not allow the combination of certain categories with others in order to attain a *nisab*, with the exception of grains and fruits. That is why one category of animals cannot be combined with another. For example, camels cannot be added to cattle to complete a *nisab*, nor can fruit be combined with raisins.

Scholars have different points of view in regard to combining various types of grains with one another. The best and the most correct opinion is that no two things can be combined to calculate a *nisab*. The *nisab* must be considered on every category by itself. This is because there are various categories and many kinds. Therefore, barley cannot be added to wheat, nor can the latter be added to the former, which is also true of dates and raisins, and chickpeas and lentils. This is the opinion of Abu Hanifah, ash-Shaf'i, and

Ahmad, according to one of the reports. Most of the early scholars hold this opinion.

Ibn al-Mundhir says that most scholars concur that camels cannot be combined with cattle or sheep, or cattle with sheep, nor dates with raisins. Thus, there can be no combining of different kinds of produce or animals. Those who allow such a practice do it without any authentic proof.

When *Zakah* is Due on Plants and Fruits

Zakah is due on plants when the grains mature and are ready to be rubbed off and on the fruit when it is ripened. In the case of dates, for example, the indication will be their brightness or red color, and with grapes their sweetness. *Zakah* becomes due only after grains are husked or the fruit becomes dried. If the farmer sold his grain after it had matured, and the fruit after it had ripened, then its *zakah* will be paid by him and not the buyer. This is because the obligation to pay *zakah* became due when the produce was still in the owner's possession.

Payment of Good (Things) for *Zakah*

Allah, the Exalted One, commanded those paying *zakah* to set it aside from the good portion of their property and forbade paying it from the bad portion. He says: "O you who believe! Spend of the good things you have earned and from that which We bring forth from the earth for you, and seek not the bad [with intent] to spend thereof [in charity] when you would not take it for yourselves save with disdain. And know that Allah is free of all wants and worthy of all praise" [*al-Baqarah*: 267].

Abu Dawud, an-Nasa'i and others reported from Sahl ibn Hanif from his father that: "The Messenger of Allah, upon whom be peace, forbade paying *zakah* with two kinds of dates called *ju'rur* and *habiq*. People used to set aside the worst of their fruit for *sadaqah* but were later on forbidden to do this by Allah: 'And seek not the bad [with intent] to spend thereof [in charity]' [*al-Baqarah*: 267]."

While mentioning this verse, al-Bara' said: "This was revealed in relation to us [al-Ansar – the Helpers], because we were owners of palm trees. A man may bring from his palm trees [dates] depending on how much he had, a cluster or two, and hang it at the mosque, and the people of the Saffah who had no food would come to the cluster and beat it with their rod. The green and unripe dates would fall off and they would eat them. There were people who did not seek good. Someone would bring a cluster of bad or inferior quality dates [*shis* and *hashaf*] or an already-broken cluster [before it had ripened] and hang it at the mosque. At this time, Allah revealed the *'ayah*: 'And seek not the bad [with intent] to spend thereof [in charity] when you would not take it for yourselves save with disdain' [*al-Baqarah*: 267]." Al-Bara' continued: "If one of you receives as a gift something similar to what he gives away, he would not accept it except out of feigned pleasure." Said al-Bara': "As a result of that, each one of us used to offer the good part of what he had." It was narrated by at-Tirmidhi who said: "It is good and sound."

In his summation of the subject, ash-Shaukani says: "This [the preceding *hadith*] means that the owner is not allowed to set aside the bad from the good on which *zakah* is due, especially in regard to dates as well as, by analogy, the various other categories on which *zakah* is due. Furthermore, the collector of *zakah* is not allowed to take it.

Zakah on Honey

Most scholars say that there is no *zakah* on honey. Al-Bukhari, for one, states: "There is no authentic tradition concerning *zakah* on honey." Ash-Shaf'i explains: "In my view, no *zakah* is levied on it because there is no evidence in the traditions (*sunan* and *'athar*) for doing so. Thus, it was exempted." Ibn al-Mundhir affirms: "There is no tradition (*khabar*) which states that *zakah* must be paid on honey, nor is there a consensus. Therefore, there is no *zakah* on honey. This is the opinion of most scholars."

The Hanafiyyah and Ahmad are of the opinion that honey is subject to *zakah*, even though there is no evidence for this view in any tradition, except for some traditions (*'athar*) which support each other. Their reason is that since it is produced from blossoms, trees, and flowers and weighed and stored like other types of produce, *zakah* is due on it. They also say it is subject to *zakah* because the cost of producing it is less than the cost of growing fruits and plants. Abu Hanifah made it a condition that when *zakah* is due on honey, it should only be collected on honey produced on tithe land. However, he did not stipulate any *nisab* for it. If this is so, then reason dictates that it should be a tithe due on any amount. Imam Ahmad, on the contrary, stipulated that it should attain a *nisab* equal to ten *'afraq*. One *faraq* equals sixteen Iraqi pounds. It makes no difference whether it is produced on *kharaj* or *'ushr* land. Abu Yusuf contends: "Its *nisab* is ten pounds but Muhammad maintains: "It is five *'afraq*." One *faraq* equals thirty-six pounds.

ZAKAH ON ANIMALS

There are authentic *ahadith* explicitly indicating that camels, cattle, and sheep are subject to *zakah*. This enjoys the consensus. There are, however, some conditions to be met:

(1) The animals concerned must attain a *nisab*. (2) They have to be in possession for one year. (3) They should have pastured by themselves — that is, grazing most of the year in the available pasture.

Most scholars agree with these conditions. Malik and al-Layth, however, say that livestock is subject to *zakah* whether it be grazing or fodder-fed, used for carrying loads or not. Nevertheless, the *ahadiths* mentioned are unequivocal in restricting *zakah* to freely grazing livestock. This suggests that there is no *zakah* on fodder-fed livestock. It is always safe to base an opinion on evidence rather than on general implications to avoid possible misunderstanding of the Prophet's intent.

Ibn 'Abdul-Barr protests: "I do not know of any jurist in the provinces who followed Malik or al-Layth in this regard."

Zakah on Camels

There is no *zakah* on camels unless there are five of them, they have been grazing freely and they have been in one's possession for a year. When the camels are five, their *zakah* is one sheep (*shah*).

[39]

When they are ten, their *zakah* is two sheep. Thus, every time they increase by five, the *zakah* due on them is one more sheep. However, when they reach twenty-five, the due *zakah* is a she-camel (*bint makhad* or *bint labun*) which is a year old and starting the second, or a young male camel which is two years and already starting the third year. When they reach thirty-six, the *zakah* due on them is a young she-camel (*bint labun*). When they reach forty-six, the due *zakah* is a she-camel (*huqqah*) which is already three years old and starting the fourth. When they reach sixty-one, the due *zakah* is a four year old camel already starting its fifth year (*jadh'ah*). When they reach seventy-six, two young she-camels (*bint labun*) are due. When they are in the range of ninety-one to 120, the *zakah* is two young camels (*huqqatan*). When the number of camels is above 120, on every forty young she-camels, one *bint labun* is due. And on every fifty above 120, a young she-camel (*huqqah*) is due.

When the ages of camels offered for *zakah* differ, the owner should pay *jadh'ah*. If he does not have it, he may pay *huqqah* and may add two sheep or twenty *dirhams* provided he can afford to. The person who has to pay *huqqah* as *zakah* but does not have it only has to pay *jadh'ah*. The *zakah* collector, then, will pay him the difference, which is twenty *dirhams* or two female sheep. The one who has to pay *huqqah* and does not possess it can pay just the *bint labun* if he has it, along with two sheep if they are available. If not, he may pay twenty *dirhams*. If he has to pay the *zakah* of *bint labun* and does not have it, he can pay a *huqqah* and will receive from the *zakah* collector twenty *dirhams* or two sheep. If he has to pay the *zakah* of *bint labun* but has only *bint makhad*, it will be accepted from him along with two sheep if they are available, or twenty *dirhams*. If he is liable for the *zakah* of bint makhad and does not possess it, a *ibn labun* will be accepted from him without any additional things. If he has only four camels, he is not supposed to pay anything unless he wants to.

These are the rules concerning *zakah* on camels which were applied by Caliph Abu Bakr as-Siddiq, and none of the companions differed with him in this matter.

Az-Zuhri reported, on the authority of Salim from his father: "The Messenger of Allah, upon whom be peace, had the rules of *sadaqah* written down but could not send them to his governors. Then, after his death, Abu Bakr dispatched them and applied them, a practice which Caliph 'Umar also followed and wanted others to follow, as indicated in his will."

Zakah on Cattle

Cattle[9] are subject to *zakah* provided they are a freely grazing herd and number thirty at the completion of the *hawl*. At that point, the *zakah* due is a young bull or a young cow (*tabi'* or *tabi'ah*). When they reach forty, the *zakah* is a young cow two years old (*musinnah*); when sixty, two young cows or two one-year-olds (*tabi'ahs*); when seventy, the *zakah* due is one *musinnah* and one *tabi'*; when eighty, two *musinnahs*; when ninety, three *tabi's*; when one hundred, one *musinnah* and two *tabi's*; when 110, two *musinnahs* and two *tabi's*; and when 120, three *musinnahs* or four *tabi's*. This system is followed on all additional cattle — one *tabi'*, and on every forty, one *musinnah*.

Zakah on Sheep (Including Goats)

Sheep are subject to *zakah* when their number reaches forty. When the herd counts forty freely grazing heads at the end of the year, its *zakah* is one sheep. This is applicable until the number reaches 120, at which point, up until 200, the *zakah* is two sheep. From 201 to 300, their *zakah* is three sheep. When the number is above 300, one additional sheep is added for each increment of one hundred. Young sheep (*jadh'*) are levied in the case of sheep and young goats (*thany*) in the case of goats. It is permissible, say scholars without exception, to levy rams as a form of *zakah* if all of the *nisab* of sheep are male. If the sheep are ewes, or a grouping of males and females, the Hanafiyyah holds it is optional to levy a *zakah* rams, whereas others specify ewes.

Regulation of *Awqas*

Definition of *Awqas*: *Awqas* is a plural form of *waqs*. A *waqs* is any amount or number that lies between the regulation of the lower ordinance and that of a higher one. Scholars agree that such a *waqs* is exempt from *zakah*. It has been confirmed in the sayings of the Prophet, upon whom be peace, concerning the *sadaqah* of camels that he said: "When the number of camels reaches twenty-five, a young she-camel one year old and already starting the second (*ibn makhad*); when they reach thirty-six to forty-five, then the *zakah* due on them is

---

[9]'Cattle' here includes camels, cows, and sheep.

a young she-camel two years old and already starting the third (*bint labun*)." Concerning the *sadaqah* of cattle, he said: "When cattle number between thirty and forty, the *zakah* is a young calf of one year old (*tabi'*) or a bull or cow of one year and already starting the second (*jadh'* or *jadh'ah*); when they reach forty, a young cow of two years old and already starting the third (*musinnah*)." Concerning *sadaqah* on sheep, he said: "When the number of freely grazing sheep is between forty-two and 120, their *zakah* is one ewe." Thus, what lies between twenty-five and thirty-six camels is considered *waqs* – that is, there is no *zakah* on them. Likewise, what lies between thirty and forty cattle is considered *waqs*. This is also applies to sheep.

What Should Not Be Included in *Zakah*

The rights of property owners must be considered when their properties are subjected to *zakah*. The best items are not to be taken as *zakah* unless the owners freely permit it. Likewise, the rights of the poor should be considered. A defective animal should not be taken as *zakah* unless all of the other animals are defective. In such a case, *zakah* is due on the average of that property. Some proofs for this view are:

(1) In the letter of Abu Bakr: "Neither an old or a defective animal nor a billy goat may be taken as *zakah*." (2) Sufyan ibn 'Abdullah ath-Thaqafi reported: "Umar forbade the *zakah* collector to levy *zakah* on the following: barren ewes (*al-'akulah*), a sheep kept at home for milk (*ar-raby*), a pregnant ewe (*al-makhid*), or a ram used for breeding (*fahl al-ghanam*)." (3) 'Abdullah ibn Mu'awiyyah al-Ghadiri reported that the Prophet, upon whom be peace, said: "Whoever performs these three acts will have had (savored) a taste of belief (*'iman*): He who worships Allah alone, and [believes] that there is no god but Him; he who good-heartedly offers the *zakah* on his property which will repay him every year; and he who does not offer a very old sheep, a mangy sheep, a sick sheep, a mean and low sheep, or a ewe which produces only a small amount of milk. You should offer one from the average. Verily, Allah asks you to offer neither the best nor the worst." It was related by Abu Dawud and at-Tabarani with a good transmission.

Zakah on Animals Other Than Cattle (al-An'am)

Zakah is not applicable to animals other than cattle. Thus, there is no *zakah* on horses, mules, or donkeys unless they are used for the purpose of trade. On the authority of 'Ali, it is related that the Prophet, upon whom be peace, said: "I have exempted you from paying *sadaqah* on horses . . ." It was narrated by Ahmad and Abu Dawud with a good chain. On the authority of Abu Hurairah, it is related that the Messenger, upon whom be peace, was asked if there is *zakah* on donkeys. He replied: "Nothing was ever mentioned [in revelation] except in the following excellent Qur'anic verse: 'And whosoever does evil equal to an atom's weight will see it' [*az-Zalzalah*: 7-8]." It was narrated by Ahmad and its details have already been mentioned.

Harithah ibn Madrab reported that he performed pilgrimage (*hajj*) with Caliph 'Umar, and the notables of Syria came to him and said: "O Commander of the Faithful, we have acquired some . . . animals, so take from our property a *sadaqah* that purifies us." He answered them: "My two predecessors [the Prophet, upon whom be peace, and Caliph Abu Bakr] did not do this before. But wait and let me ask the Muslims about this." This was narrated by al-Haythami, who said that it was narrated by Ahmad and at-Tabarani in the book entitled *al-Kabir*. The narrators of this *hadith* are considered trustworthy.

Az-Zuhri reported from Salman ibn Yassar that the people of Syria said to Abu 'Ubaidah ibn al-Jarrah: "Take from our horses . . . a *sadaqah*." He refused. Then he wrote to 'Umar, who also refused. They spoke to him again, and he wrote to 'Umar once again. 'Umar wrote back: "If they desire that, take it from them and give it back to them [their poor] and to their slaves." This was narrated by Malik and al-Baihaqi.

Young Camels, Calves, and Lambs

When a person has a *nisab* of camels, cattle, and lambs, and they give birth during the same year, *zakah* is due on both the original number and their offsprings at the end of the year. Their *zakah* is considered a lump-sum *zakah* according to the majority of scholars. On the authority of Malik and ash-Shaf'i, from Sufyan ibn 'Abdullah ath-Thaqafi, it is related that 'Umar ibn al-Khattab said: "The new-born sheep (*as-sakhlah*) carried by the shepherd are not to be taken as *zakah*. Likewise, a barren sheep (*al-'akulah*), a ewe kept for milk (*ar-raby*), a pregnant ewe (*al-makhid*) and a ram used for breeding (*fahl al-ghanam*) are not to be taken as *zakah*. Take as *zakah* the *jadh'ah* and the *thaniyyah*. Zakah is levied on the average quality of the property."

Abu Hanifah, ash-Shaf'i, and Abu Thaur are of the opinion that the young offspring are not to be calculated in the *zakah* payment unless the mature animals make a *nisab*. Also, Abu Hanifah stated that the young sheep can be added to fulfill a *nisab* whether they are born from the same livestock or not. They will be subject to *zakah* at the end of the year. Ash-Shaf'i lays down the condition that young animals have to be born prior to the completion of the *nisab*. There is no *zakah* on young animals according to Abu Hanifah, Muhammad, Dawud, ash-Shu'abi, and Ahmad.

Ahmad, Abu Dawud, an-Nasa'i, ad-Daraqutni and al-Baihaqi, relate that Suwaid ibn Ghaflah said: "The *zakah* collector of the Messenger of Allah, upon whom be peace, came to us and I heard him say: 'In my term of office, a suckling animal was not subject to *zakah* ...'" In its chain of narrators is Hilal ibn Hubab, whom several have declared trustworthy, but some did not. It was authenticated by more than one person but was a point of contention to others.

According to the opinion of Malik and a report from Ahmad, young animals as well as mature ones are subject to *zakah*, because if the former could be considered with others (for purposes of *zakah*), then they could also be considered on their own. Ash-Shaf'i and Abu Yusuf hold that at least one young (animal) is obligatory (as *zakah*) from the young animals.

On Combining Young and Old (Animals) or Separating Them

1) Suwaid ibn Ghaflah said: "The *zakah* collector of the Messenger of Allah, upon whom be peace, came to us and I heard him say: 'We do not collect *zakah* on suckling animals, nor do we separate between them [young and old], nor combine them together.' A man came with a great humped camel (*kawma*), but he did not accept it as *zakah*." It was reported by Ahmad, Abu Dawud and an-Nasa'i.

2) Anas reported that Abu Bakr wrote to him: "These are the *sadaqah* stipulations which the Messenger of Allah, upon whom be peace, made obligatory to the Muslims. [And of it] do not combine. There is no need to gather [young and old] animals nor to separate them to obtain the correct *sadaqah* amount. What happens to a mixture of young and old? When *zakah* is assessed on two associates, then they have to figure it out equally among them." Al-Bukhari relates this.

Malik, in *al-Muwattā'*, says: "There are, for example, three partners, each having forty sheep on which *zakah* is payable. If they add their sheep together, their *zakah* will be only one sheep. Or, another example: two partners have 201 sheep. Their *zakah* will be three sheep. If they divide the flock among them, their *zakah* will be one sheep each."

Ash-Shaf'i holds that this statement is addressed to both the owner and the *zakah* collector. Each is ordered not to add or separate his possessions to obtain a lower or higher *sadaqah*. Since the owner would naturally prefer a low *sadaqah* on his property, he would combine or separate his possessions accordingly. The same would also be true of the *zakah* collector, who might like to collect as much *sadaqah* as possible. By using the phrase *khashyat as-sadaqah* (for fear of *sadaqah*), the Prophet meant that it may become more or less since both alternatives were possible. This shows that he did not prefer one choice over the other. Therefore, he made both alternatives possible. According to the Hanafiyyah: "This is, in a sense, a prohibition on the *zakah* collector's separating the property of a person so that his *sadaqah* is not increased. For example: a man possesses 120 sheep. If they are divided into three lots of forty each, the *zakah* would amount to three sheep. Another example: if they combine the property of one man with the property of another, the *sadaqah* would increase. Thus, if a person owns 101 sheep and another owns an equal number, then the *zakah* collector, if he combines the two lots, would secure three sheep as payment toward *zakah*, while the actual amount due is only two sheep."

Does Combining (Animals) Have any Effect?

The Hanafiyyah hold that as far as the determination of *zakah* is concerned, combining (animals) has no effect. Whether such a combination is between partners or has ensued because of contiguity does not matter. There will be no *zakah* on the joint ownership of partners unless each of them attains a *nisab*. The consensus is that *zakah* has to be determined on the basis of sole ownership.

The Malikiyyah maintain that ownership of cattle is considered as one for the purpose of *zakah*. The combination becomes valid only for *zakah* when the co-owners in their own right possess a *nisab*. In addition to this, they should have a common herdsman, a common breed, a common pen, and the expressed intention of having joint ownership. If the herd of one of them is distinguished from the other, they will be considered two separate entities. In that case, each individual becomes liable for *zakah*. The combination affects livestock. What is taken as *zakah* from the herd will be distributed among the partners in accordance with each one's share. If the property of one of the associates is separate, then all of it is considered combined.

According to the Shaf'iyyah, every share of the combination affects the *zakah* and the *zakah* on two or more associates' separate properties becomes due. This may affect the amount of *zakah* due; for example, if two men, each possessing twenty sheep, combine their sheep, the *zakah* due is one, but if they do not combine them, then there is no *zakah* on either one. On the other hand, a combination of 101 sheep with the same number results in a *zakah* of one and one-half sheep. However, if the flocks of sheep are considered separately, then the *zakah* due on each lot is only one sheep. As for the case of three associates, each of them having forty sheep, if they combine them, the *zakah* due is one sheep — that is, the *zakah* due for each partner is one-third of a sheep. However, if treated separately, each should pay one sheep. In addition to this, the Shaf'iyyah moreover stipulate the following:

(1) The partners should qualify financially to pay *zakah*. (2) The combined property must attain a *nisab*. (3) Its *zakah* is due at the end of the year. (4) None of the properties is singled out from the others as regards resting pen, grazing area, watering, herdsmen, and milking sheds. (5) Flocks of the same kind are bred by the same ram.

Ahmad agrees with the Shaf'iyyah, except that he limited the effect of combination to cattle and does not take into consideration any other properties.

ZAKAH ON BURIED TREASURE AND PRECIOUS MINERALS

The term *rikāz* is etymologically derived from *rakaza*, the perfect tense of the verb *yarkuzu* (the imperfect root). It means 'to be hidden.' Allah, the Exalted One, says: "Or hear from them the slightest sound" [*Maryam*: 98] — that is, *rikz* means a slight sound.

In the present context, this refers to what was buried at the time of *jahiliyyah* (the pre-Islamic period). Malik and many other scholars are of the opinion that *rikāz* means objects buried before the Arabs embraced Islam and which were dug up without any expensive effort or money. If these conditions cannot be met, then it is not considered *rikāz*. Abu Hanifah holds that it is a name of an entity hidden either by the Creator or by the created one (man).

The Meaning of Minerals and Their Conditions for *Zakah*

The term *ma'din* (minerals) is derived from the verb *'adana* (to reside), as in the phrase "*'adana fi al-makan*," which means 'someone resided in some place.' Allah, the Exalted One, says: "Allah has promised to the believing men and believing women gardens of Eden" [*at-Taubah*: 72] since it is an abode for eternity.

Scholars differ about minerals (*ma'din*) which are subject to *zakah*. Ahmad holds that everything dug from the ground, whether created in it or buried by man, and which has a value (such as gold, silver, iron, copper, lead, sapphires, chrysolite, emeralds, turquoise, crystal, agate, kohl (antimony sulfide), arsenic, tar, petroleum, sulphur, *zaj*) are subject to *zakah*. He, however, made it a condition that the extracted mineral should attain a *nisab* either by itself or by its value. Abu Hanifah is of the opinion that *zakah* is payable on any mineral that can receive an imprint or melt by fire, such as gold, silver, iron, or copper. As for liquids such as tar, or a solid mineral which cannot be melted by fire such as rubies, there is no *zakah* on them. In the former case, the admissibility of *nisab* is not a prior condition. Whether large or small in amount, a fifth will be taken as *zakah*.

Malik and ash-Shaf'i hold that both gold and silver qualify for *zakah*. Like Ahmad, they insist that the gold should weigh at least twenty *mithqal* (a weight equal to 4.68 g.) and the silver at least 200 *dirhams*. They agree (with the Hanafiyyah) that these metals do not require completion of a year to be subjected to *zakah*, which becomes due anytime it is available. According to the preceding scholars, the amount should be one-fortieth, and its distribution should be like that of the regular *zakah*. For Abu Hanifah, its distribution is similar to booty (*fay'*).

The Legitimacy of *Zakah* on *Rikāz* and *Ma'din*

That *zakah* of *rikāz* and *ma'din* is obligatory is shown by a statement attributed to Abu Hurairah: "The Prophet, upon whom be peace, said: 'There is no compensation for one killed or wounded by an animal, falling in a well, or because of working in mines; but, one-fifth (*khums*) is compulsory on *rikaz*.' " Ibn al-Mundhir confesses that he does not know anyone who contradicted this *hadith* except al-Hasan, who differentiates between what exists in the land of war and the Islamic land. The latter holds that if *rikaz* is found in the land of war, one-fifth (*khums*) is due, but if it is found in the Islamic land, it will be subject to the regular *zakah*.

Explaining it, Ibn al-Qayyim says that there are two interpretations of this statement:

The first interpretation is that whenever someone hires someone else to dig a mine for him and then he falls into it and is killed, there is no compensation for him. This view is supported by the Prophet's saying: "There is no compensation for one who falls into a well or who is killed by an animal – (*al-bi'r jubar, wa al-'ajma' jubar*)."

The second interpretation is that there is no *zakah* on minerals. This view is supported by the Prophet's saying: "... but one-fifth is compuslory on treasure — (*wa fi az-zakah al-khums*)." Thus, he differentiated between mineral (*ma'din*) and treasure (*rikaz*). He made *zakah* on *rikaz* compulsory because it is a wealth obtained without any cost or effort. He exempted minerals (*ma'din*) from *zakah* because they require both cost and effort for their mining.

Rikāz Upon Which *Zakah* is Paid

The *rikaz* are all those substances upon which one-fifth (*khums*) is payable, such as gold, silver, iron, lead, brass, and the like. This is the opinion of the Hanafiyyah, the Hanbaliyyah, Ishaq, and Ibn al-Mundhir. A report from Malik and one of the two opinions of ash-Shaf'i also corroborate it. Ash-Shaf'i also holds that only gold and silver are subject to *khums*.

The Location of *Rikāz*

Rikāz might be found in the following places: 1. In a barren land, a land of unknown ownership, or in an intractible road, or ruined village. In that case, *khums* has to be paid, and the one who found it may keep the other four-fifths for himself. This is based on a report from an-Nasa'i on the authority of 'Amr ibn Shu'aib from his father and from his grandfather, who said that when the Messenger of Allah, upon whom be peace, was asked about a lucky find (*al-luqatah*), he responded: "For anything along a tractable road or in an inhabited village, its ownership is determined by established custom. If the owner claims it, it is his. However, when an item is found in an intractable road or in an uninhabited village, then on it and the rest of the find, one-fifth (*khums*) is payable."

2. If the *rikāz* is found by someone in a land transferred to him, then it is his, as it is lodged in the land. Nevertheless, his ownership does not come from his possession of the land — it comes from the fact that it became known to him. Analogically, this kind of find falls into the category of grass, firewood, and game which are found on land which is not his. He can claim it if the one who transferred the land does not ask for it. In that case, it will be his because the land originally belonged to him. This is the view of Abu Yusuf, and the Hanbaliyyah uphold it as sound. Ash-Shaf'i says it belongs to the owner who transferred the land (if he claims it) before him, and so on until it is claimed by the first original owner.

Whenever land is transferred through inheritance, it is considered an inheritance by itself. If, however, the inhabitants agree that it did not belong to the one from whom they inherited it, then it belongs to the original owner. If he is unknown, then it is considered the lost property of an unknown owner. Abu Hanifah and Muhammad say that it belongs to the original owner of the land or to his inheritors if they are known; if they are not, it is to be placed in the public treasury.

3. If it is found in the land of a Muslim or a free non-Muslim subject (*dhimmi*), then it belongs to the owner of the land, according to Abu Hanifah, Muhammad, and Ahmad. It is also reported from Ahmad that it belongs to the one who found it (*rikāz*). Al-Hasan ibn Salih, Abu Thaur, and Abu Yusuf also preferred this opinion. This view is based on the belief that *rikāz* is not necessarily owned by the owner of the land, except when it is claimed by the owner. In such a case, his word will be the final one because he has the right over the land. If he does not claim it, it belongs to the one who finds it. Ash-Shaf'i holds that it belongs to the one who claims it. Otherwise, it belongs to the original owner.

The Amount Payable on *Rikāz*

The amount payable on *rikāz* is one-fifth, regardless of a *nisab*, according to Abu Hanifah, Ahmad, and one of the two correct reports of Malik and ash-Shaf'i. As for the completion of a year (*hawl*), all scholars agree that it has not been stipulated as a conditon.

Who Must Pay the *Khums* (One-Fifth)

Most scholars are of the opinion that *khums* is due on anyone who finds a treasure, whether he happens to be a Muslim, a free non-Muslim subject (*dhimmi*), old, young, sane, or insane. However, the guardians of the young and insane must pay it on their behalf. Ibn al-Mundhir comments that all learned persons agree that a *dhimmi* who finds *rikaz* has to pay its *khums*. This is also the opinion of Malik, the scholars of Madinah, ath-Thauri, al-Auza'i, the scholars of Iraq, those who use analogy (*ashab ar-ra'y*), and others. Ash-Shaf'i stated that *khums* is only due upon those who must pay *zakah*.

Distribution of *Khums*

According to ash-Shaf'i, the distribution of *khums* is similar to the distribution of *zakah*. Ahmad and al-Baihaqi narrate from Bishr al-Khath'ami that a man from his tribe said: "While I was in Kufah, I received a jar from an old monastery at the *zakah* district (*jibayah*) of Bishr. There were 4,000 *dirhams* in it. I took it to 'Ali, who told me to divide it into five parts, which I did. Then, 'Ali took one-fifth and gave me four-fifths. When I departed, he called me and asked if there were some needy people living near me. I replied that there were, and he asked me to divide the one-fifth among them." Abu Hanifah, Malik, and Ahmad are of the opinion that its distribution is similar to the distribution of booty (*fay'*).

Ash-Shu'bi narrates that a man, while he was out of Madinah, found 1,000 *dinars* in the ground. He brought them to 'Umar ibn al-Khattab, who took the *khums* of 200 *dinars* and gave the man the rest. 'Umar started to distribute the 200 *dinars* among the Muslims who were present. Since a little bit was left over, he then asked: "Where is the owner of the *dinars*?" When the man responded, 'Umar said to him: "Take these *dinars*, for they are yours." In *al-Mughni*, it says that if it were like *zakah*, he would have alloted it to those who deserved it and would not have returned it to its finder. Furthermore, *rikaz* can be given to the *dhimmi*, whereas *zakah* is not.

ZAKAH ON WEALTH
EXTRACTED FROM THE SEA

Most scholars stipulate that *zakah* is not payable on anything extracted from the sea, such as pearls, corals, chrysalite, cachalot's ambergris, fish, and so on. There is, however, a report from Ahmad that if the amount extracted reaches a *nisab*, then *zakah* is due on it. Abu Yusuf agrees with him in the case of pearls and cachalot's ambergris. Ibn 'Abbas holds that there is no *zakah* of cachalot, beacause it is an object thrown out by the sea. Jabir said that there is no *zakah* on cachalot, but that it is a free spoil for anyone who finds it.

Acquiring Property Through Profit or Increase

When a person acquires property and it stays in his possession for a year and constitutes a *nisab*, and he has no other property or he has similar property which has not reached a *nisab* except when the acquired property has been added to it, then the year *hawl* of *zakah* becomes applicable to it from the time of its acquisition. The *zakah* will be payable at the completion of the *hawl*. In such a case, the acquired property may be classified in any of the following categories:

1. The acquired holdings increase in value either by profits from trade or by an increase in animal production. These kinds of holdings qualify themselves for the application of the *hawl* and

zakah. For the individual whose merchandise or animals constitute
a *nisab* and whose business also makes a profit or whose animals
reproduce during the course of the *hawl*, he should count the original and additional property as one for the purpose of *zakah*. There
is no dispute about this among scholars.

2. As for the acquired property which falls under the same
category as the attained *nisab* but is not derived or generated from
it — that is, it was acquired through purchase, gift, or inheritance —
Abu Hanifah holds that this may be combined with the *nisab* in
order to become a part of it with regard to the *hawl* and payment of
zakah. Thus, the principal property and the profits are collectively
taxable.

Ash-Shaf'i and Ahmad suggest that newly acquired property
be combined with the original one for the purpose of attaining a
nisab and that a new *hawl* has to be assumed for it — whether the
original consists of cash or animals. For example, if someone has 200
dirhams and manages to acquire another 200 *dirhams* during the
year, he should pay *zakah* on both at the completion of the *hawl*
which will begin to roll at the acquisition of new property. Malik's
opinion is like that of Abu Hanifah's concerning animals but like
Ahmad's in regard to gold and silver.

3. The acquired holdings are not of the same kind that one
already possesses. As such, they cannot be combined with the original either for the *nisab* or for the year count (*hawl*). If, however, the
acquired holdings by themselves reach a *nisab*, their year count will
be calculated independently, and the owner will pay their *zakah* at
the completion of the *hawl*. In the absence of these conditions, nothing is applicable to these holdings. This is the opinion of the majority of scholars.

Zakah is the Responsibility of the Owner, Not the Holdings Themselves

The Hanafiyyah, the Malikiyyah, and a report from ash-Shaf'i
and Ahmad propose that it is the property which owes *zakah*. The
second opinion attributed to ash-Shaf'i and Ahmad is that *zakah* is
the responsibility of the owner, not the property. The difference
between the two opinions is obvious:

For example, someone had 200 *dirhams* and did not pay *zakah*
on the sum for two years. The opinion which says that *zakah* is due
on the property itself means that the amount due is for one year
only since it decreased by five *dirhams*, which was the amount due

for *zakah* at the end of the first year. The second opinion, that *zakah* is the responsibility of the owner, means that he should pay *zakah* twice, one for each year, as *zakah* is the responsibility of the owner and is not affected by the decrease of the *nisab*.

Ibn Hazm favors the view that it is the owner's responsibility. There has been no difference of opinion, he says, among the Muslims since the time of the Prophet, upon whom be peace, down to his time as to the applicability of *zakah* on wheat, barley, dates, silver, gold, camels, cattle, and sheep. Concerning payment of *zakah* from a different lot of wheat, barley, dates, gold, silver, camels, cattle, and sheep, he says it does not matter whether one pays it from the same lot, from a different one in one's possession, or from a lot that may be bought, granted as a gift, or borrowed.

The conviction that the payment of *zakah* is the owner's responsibility and is not necessarily that of the property itself is a sound principle, for if it becomes due on the property itself, the owner will not be permitted to make payment from a different lot. It is similar to the case of one partner being prevented from giving his money to his copartner from a source other than the one involved in their partnership — unless the partners approve of it and it does not violate the conditions of the transaction between them. Furthermore, if *zakah* has to be applied to the property itself, only two situations can arise. First, *zakah* is payable on all parts of that property and is applicable to any individual amount of it, without individual specification. Second, if it is applicable to every part of it, it is impermissible to sell from any herd or grain since *zakah* collectors in this case would become partners. Thus, the proprietor is not allowed to take anything from it. This is void without any dispute. Furthermore, it would become obligatory upon him to specify exactly the price of the sheep which he desires to take out, just as is done in partnerships. If *zakah* is due on any part of it other than the property itself, it becomes void. This holds true in such a case since he does not know what he might sell or whether he is taking what is due for the *sadaqah* collectors. This, in turn, backs up the above.

Loss of the Holdings after *Zakah* is Due

Once *zakah* becomes payable on the holdings either because of the completion of a year or harvest time, and the holdings or part of them are lost, the owner still has to pay it. Whether the loss occured owing to negligence or not does not matter.

This is the opinion of Ibn Hazm and the better opinion of the Hanbaliyyah. Abu Hanifah holds that it vitiates the payment of *zakah* if all the property perishes without the owner's role in its destruction. When part of it perishes, the perished portion is not subject to *zakah*. This is in accordance with the rule that *zakah* is associated with the property itself. However, when the property is deliberately destroyed by the owner, *zakah* has to be paid. Ash-Shaf'i, al-Hassan ibn Salih, Ishaq, Abu Thaur, and Ibn al-Mundhir hold that if the *nisab* perishes before *zakah* is paid, then the owner owes nothing. However, if it perishes subsequent to the accumulation of the *nisab*, the owner has to pay it. Ibn Qudamah supports this view and says it vitiates the payment of *zakah* if the property perishes without any negligence on the part of the owner. This is because it is obligatory for the sake of beneficence, which presupposes the existence of the property — and not with the purpose of impoverishing the payers of *zakah*.

Negligence in this context implies that the owner had accumulated the *nisab* and thus it was possible for him to pay *zakah*, but he did not and the property perished. On the contrary, if he did not have the *nisab*, or the holdings were not in his possession, or they were to be purchased and he could not, then this does not constitute an act of negligence.

Likewise, if it is presumed that the obligation to pay *zakah* remains even after the holdings are lost, and the owner has the means to pay it, then he must do so. Otherwise, he should be granted a respite in order to fulfill his obligation to pay *zakah*. This is akin to a debt one owes to someone but the debt owed to Allah should be considered more important.

The Loss of *Zakah* After it is Set Aside

When a person sets aside *zakah* for distribution among the poor and all of it or some of it is lost, he must repay it because it is still his responsibility.

Ibn Hazm says: "We received a narration from Ibn Abi Shaibah on the authority of Hafs ibn Ghayath, Jarir, al-Mu'tamir ibn Sulaiman at-Taymi, Zaid ibn al-Hubab, and 'Abdulwahhab ibn 'Ata; also from Hafs, who narrated on the authority of Hisham ibn Hassan from al-Hassan al-Basri; Jarir who reported, on the authority of al-Mughirah from his companions; and al-Mu'tamir who reported from Mu'amar from Hammad; and Zaid who reported from Shu'bah from al-Hakam; and 'Abdulwahhab who reported on the authority of Ibn Abi 'Urubah from Hammad from Ibrahim an-Nakha'i that whoever sets aside *zakah* from his property and then it is lost, his obligation to pay *zakah* still remains to be discharged, and he must set it aside again."

There exists, however, another opinion on it: "We received a narration on the authority of 'Ata' that the obligation will be discharged [if set aside and lost]," says Ibn Hazm.

Delaying of *Zakah* (Payment) Does Not Void it

Ash-Shaf'i holds that anyone who does not pay *zakah* for a number of years must pay it all together. Whether or not he is aware of its obligation or he happens to be in a Muslim or non-Muslim land, makes no difference. Based on the opinion of Malik, ash-Shaf'i and Abu Thaur, Ibn al-Mundhir says: "When unjust people rule a country and the people of that country do not pay their *zakah* for a number of years, then their new leader should take it from them."

The Payment of the Value Instead of Paying the Item Itself

It is not permissible to pay the value instead of the item itself, except in the case of non-existence, for *zakah* is an act of worship which can only be fulfilled according to the specified manner, with the rich sharing their wealth with the poor

Mu'adh reported that the Prophet, upon whom be peace, sent him to Yemen and told him: "Take grain from grain, sheep from sheep, camels from camels, and cows from cows." This *hadith* is narrated by Abu Dawud, Ibn Majah, al-Baihaqi, and al-Hakim. It should be noted that there is an interruption in the chain of this *hadith*, since 'Ata' did not hear it from Mu'adh.

Disapproving of substitution, ash-Shaukani says: "The truth of the matter is that *zakah* is obligatory on the item itself and should not be substituted for its value except where there is a valid excuse."

Abu Hanifah permits the acceptance of the value whether the individual owing could pay it in the items itself or not because *zakah* is the right of the poor, and he believed that it made no difference whether it was paid in the item or in something else of equal value. Al-Bukhari reports, with a firm statement, that Mu'adh asked the people of Yemen to give him either goods or clothes of silk or garments as *zakah* instead of barley and corn because it was more convenient for them. The companions of the Prophet, upon whom be peace, were also given the choice in Madinah.

Zakah on Shared Property

When holdings are shared between two or more partners, *zakah* is not obligatory on either one until all of them attain a *nisab* individually. This is the opinion of most scholars. This does not include the combination of animals, which has been discussed earlier.

Evading the Payment of *Zakah*

The opinion of Malik, al-Auza'i, Ishaq, Ahmad, and Abu 'Ubaid is that whoever possesses a *nisab* of any kind of property and then sells it before the completion of the year *hawl*, or gives it away as a gift, or damages part of it with the intention of avoiding its *zakah*, he still must pay its *zakah*. If he engages himself in any of the preceding acts at a time when his obligation to pay *zakah* is about to mature, he will be forced to pay it. If, however, any of the preceding acts happen at the beginning of the *hawl*, this will not constitute an evasion, and he will be (legally) free from his obligation to pay *zakah*.

Abu Hanifah and ash-Shaf'i hold that since the amount decreased before the end of the *hawl*, *zakah* will not be paid on it. He would still be considered a wrongdoer and disobedient to Allah for attempting to escape it. The early Muslims based their rationale on the *'ayahs* in which Allah, the Exalted One, says: "Lo! We have tried them as We tried the owners of the garden when they vowed they would pluck its fruit the next morning, and made no reservation [for the will of Allah]. Then a visitation from your Lord came upon it while they were asleep. So the garden became a dark and desolate spot in the morning, as if it were plucked" [*al-Mulk*: 17-20]. Allah punished those people for avoiding their obligation to the poor.

Zakah, as such, will still be due and the person has to pay it because his intention was to deprive the poor of their share in his wealth. This would be similar to the case of a man who divorces his wife during his terminal illness. His evil intention calls for punishment as a redemptive act. Another case of a similar nature would be that of a person who kills his benefactor so that he could have his inheritance. In that case, Allah punishes him by depriving him of his inheritance.

THE RECIPIENTS OF ZAKAH

There are eight categories of the beneficiaries of *zakah* which Allah specifies in the Qur'an: "The alms are only for the poor and the needy, for those who collect them, for those whose hearts are to be reconciled, for the freedom of those who are captives and in debt, for the cause of Allah, and for the wayfarers; [it is] a duty imposed by Allah. Allah is the Knower, the Wise" [*at-Taubah*: 60]. Ziyad ibn al-Harith as-Suda'i reported: "I came to the Messenger of Allah, upon whom be peace, and pledged allegience to him. Then a man came and said to the Messenger: 'Give me some of the collected *sadaqah*.' The Messenger replied: 'Allah did not leave the matter of *sadaqat* to be decided by a prophet nor to others ... He Himself classified it into eight categories. If you fit into any of these categories, I will give you your due.'" It was narrated by Abu Dawud although in its chain of transmission there is 'Abdurrahman al-'Afriqi, who is of questionable merits.

The following is an elaboration upon the preceding eight categories:

I. **The Poor** (*al-Fuqāra'*).

II. **The Needy** (*al-Masākīn*): The needy, along with the poor mentioned above, are those who do not even have basic needs fulfilled. This categroy parallels the category of the rich who have all they need. As mentioned elsewhere, a person is considered rich if he possesses the *nisab* — that is, an amount in excess of his essential needs or those of

[59]

his children with regard to food, drink, clothing, housing, animals, tools of his trade, and similar other necessities. Thus, one who lacks all these is considered poor (*fuqura'*) and qualifies for *zakah.*

A *hadith* attributed to Mu'adh instructs: "Take from the rich [that is those who are self-sufficient] and give to their poor." Thus, *zakah* should be taken from the rich who own a *nisab* and given to those who are not so fortunate.

No difference has been made here between the poor (*fuqura'*) and the needy (*masakin*) as far as their needs, their poverty, and their qualification for receiving *zakah* are concerned. The two are brought together in the preceding Qur'anic *'ayah* with the necessary conjunction so that they could be differentiated from each other. This does not contradict our categorizing the *masakin* as a subgroup of the *fuqura'.* In the following *hadith*, the text indicates that the needy are the poor who are not noticed by the people because they abstain from begging. The Qur'an takes note of them because they, perhaps due to their modesty, go unnoticed.

Abu Hurairah reported that the Messenger of Allah, upon whom be peace, said: "The needy person (*miskin*) is not one who goes around asking the people for a date or two, or for a mouthful or two, but the one who is too embarrassed to ask. Read if you wish: 'They do not beg from men importunately' [*al-Baqarah*: 273]." In a variant of this report, it is related: "The needy person is not one who goes around asking people for a mouthful or two or a date or two, but the one who has not enough [money] to satisfy his needs and whose condition is not known to others. Thus, *sadaqah* is given to him and he does not beg from the people." This is narrated by al-Bukhari and Muslim.

The amount of zakah given to a poor person: *Zakah* aims at supporting the poor by satisfying their needs. A specified amount is therefore given to them on a continuous basis to alleviate their state of poverty. This amount differs depending on circumstances and individuals. 'Umar reported: "If you happen to give [alms], you should give to satisfy one's needs." Qadi 'Abdulwahhab says that Malik never stipulated a limit to the amount that can be given. To him, *zakah* may even be given to one who has a house, a servant, and a mount to ride, provided he is in need. The import of the preceding *hadith* is clear — that is, asking for help is permissible for a person who is poor until he gets what he needs for his livelihood and is freed from his needs.

Qabisah ibn Mukhariq al-Hilali reported: "I had a debt. I went to the Messenger of Allah, upon whom be peace, and asked for his help. He answered: 'Wait until we have funds for *sadaqah*, then we will give you some.' He also said: 'O Qabisah, *sadaqah* is justified only for the following three: first, a man who is in debt, for his case makes it permissible to receive [alms] until his difficulty is resolved; second, a man who is struck by calamity which destroys his holdings, which also makes it permissible for him to receive [alms] until he is in a position to earn a sustenance [or he said, '. . . what satisfies his needs and makes him self-sufficient']; and third, a man who has been reduced to poverty and three persons of caliber from among his people testify to his desperate situation will receive until he finds for himself a means of support [or he said, '. . . what satisfies his needs and makes him self-sufficient']. Other than these cases, O Qabisah, it is not permissible (*sahat*). A person receiving it (*sadaqah*) will be consuming forbidden holdings.' " This is narrated by Ahmad, Muslim, Abu Dawud, and an-Nasa'i.

Is *zakah* given to a person who can work?: Individuals strong in body and earning their living are not entitled to *zakah*. Their position is similar to that of the rich.

(1) 'Ubaidullah ibn 'Adiyy al-Khiyar reported: "Two men told me that they went to the Prophet, upon whom be peace, during the Farewell Pilgrimage while he was distributing charity. They asked him for help. He gave them a look from the head down and then found them to be sturdy and strong. Then he said: 'If you desire, I shall give it to you. But, there is no *zakah* for one who is rich, neither for the one who is strong and earning.' " This is related by Abu Dawud and an-Nasa'i.

Concerning the merits of this *hadith*, al-Khattabi says that it provides the criterion that if a person is not known to have means, it will be presumed that he has none. The *hadith* also provides the rule that one who appears to be sturdy is not excluded from receiving the *zakah* unless his income is determined, for there are some people who are strong in body but for one reason or another are unable to work. Such people may receive charity according to this *hadith*.

(2) It is related from Rayhan ibn Yazid from 'Abdullah ibn 'Amr that the Prophet, upon whom be peace, said: "*Sadaqah* is neither permissible for the rich nor for the one who is of energetic disposition, sound body, and healthy limbs." This is related by Abu Dawud and at-Tirmidhi. The latter grades it as sound (*sahih*). Ash-Shaf'i, Ishaq, Abu 'Ubaid, and Ahmad uphold it. The Hanafiyyah say a strong and healthy person is allowed to take *sadaqah*, provided he does not possess 200 *dirhams* or more. An-Nawawi says: "I asked al-Ghazzali if an able-bodied person who comes from a rich family and is not used to

physical labor in earning his living can be entitled to *zakah*. He answered that he could." This is a sound rule which takes into consideration a person's vocation.

The owner who lacks self-sufficiency: One whose possessions reach a *nisab* but are still insufficient for his needs, due to the size of his family or the high cost of living, will be considered well-off and subject to *zakah*. He is also considered poor because his possessions are not enough for his needs. As such, he should also be given *zakah*. An-Nawawi says that one who possesses a piece of real estate but does not have enough income to meet his needs should be considered poor and eligible for that amount of *zakah* which would satisfy his needs. In this way, he would not have to sell his real estate. *Al-Mughni* mentions that al-Maymum said: "I had a talk with Abu 'Abdullah, Ahmad ibn Hanbal and I said: 'A man may possess camels and sheep on which *zakah* is due and be considered poor. He may possess forty sheep or even a landed estate (*day'ah*), not enough for his needs. Would he be allowed to receive alms?' He answered: 'Yes, because he does not possess what is sufficient for him and he is not able to earn what he needs. In that case, he is permitted to receive *zakah*, if what he possesses does not qualify for *zakah*.' "

III. Collectors of *Zakah*: *Zakah* collectors are officials appointed by the leader or his deputy to collect it from the rich. Among them are the custodians of *zakah*, shepherds and clerks for its administration. They must be Muslims and should consist of those who are potentially not eligible for *zakah*. This includes the family of the Prophet – that is, Banu 'Abdul Mutallib. It is related by al-Muttalib ibn Rabi'ah ibn Harith ibn 'Abdul Muttalib that he and al-Fadl ibn al-'Abbas went to the Messenger of Allah, upon whom be peace: "One of us said: 'O Messenger of Allah! We have come to you so that you may invest us with authority to administer *zakah*, that we shall gather (collect) the benefits the people are to receive, and render service to you that others give.' The Messenger of Allah answered: 'Indeed, *zakah* ought not to be given to Muhammad or to the family of Muhammad. *Zakah* is nothing but filth that comes out from people's properties.' " This is reported by Ahmad and Muslim. Another version states: "It is not permitted to Muhammad or to the family of Muhammad."

Certain people, though well-off, can still receive *zakah*: Abu Sa'id reported that the Prophet, upon whom be peace, said: "*Sadaqah* is not allowed for the well-off except for the following five: an administrator of *zakah*, a purchaser of *zakah* holdings, a debtor, a warrior in the cause of Allah, or a person who is given a present by the needy (*miskīn*) from what the latter had been granted as *zakah*." This is related by Ahmad, Abu Dawud, Ibn Majah, and al-Hakim. The latter grades the preceding *hadith* as sound according to the criteria of Muslim and al-Bukhari.

What *zakah* collectors take from *zakah* is their wages for work done: 'Abdullah ibn as-Sa'di related that he came from Syria to see 'Umar ibn al-Khattab, who asked him: "Is it true that you perform a certain job for the Muslims and you are given wages for that, but you do not accept them?" He answered: "Yes, indeed. I possess horses and slaves. I am well-off. I want my work to be a charity for the Muslims." Then 'Umar said: "I also wanted what you desired, but the Prophet, upon whom be peace, used to pay compensation to me. I would say to him: 'Give it to one who is poorer than I.' Once he gave me money and I said to him: 'Give it to a person more needy than I.' Then the Prophet, upon whom be peace, said: 'Take what Allah, to Whom belongs might and majesty, gives you of His bounties without your having asked for it or being eager.' So take it and keep it, or give it away as charity — and what is not given should not be asked for." This is related by al-Bukhari and an-Nasa'i.

The wages ought to be sufficient to cover legitimate needs: Al-Mustawrid ibn Shaddad relates that the Prophet, upon whom be peace, said: "If someone performed a job for us and has no house, let him have a house; if he has no wife, let him have a wife; if he has no servant, let him have a servant; or if he has no mount to ride, let him have one. He who clamors for anything other than these is being excessive." This is related by Ahmad and Abu Dawud and its chain is sound. Commenting on the subject, al-Khattabi says: "This may be interpreted in two different ways. The first means that the individual is permitted to have a servant or a house deducted from his wages, which are similar to any other wages. He is not permitted to take anything else. The second means that the *zakah* worker has the right to have lodging and a servant. Thus, if he does not have a house or a servant, one may be hired to serve him and a house may be rented for him during the tenure of his job."

IV. Reconcilation of hearts: This applies primarily to that group of people whose hearts, due to their weak Islam, need to be reconciled or strengthened for Islam. In this case, *zakah* is distributed to rid Muslims of their evil, or to procure their assistance in the defense of Muslims. The jurists divide such people into Muslims and unbelievers. The Muslims are divided into four groups:

(1) Leaders: People who are leaders and notables among the Muslims and influential among their nonbelieving kinsmen deserve and if given *sadaqah*, there is hope that their kinsmen will become Muslims. Such was the case of Abu Bakr giving 'Adiyy ibn Hatim and az-Zibarqan ibn Badr *sadaqah* because of their high status among their people.

(2) Recently converted prominent people: Prominent people among Muslims, though recently converted to Islam and as such of weak faith but still obeyed by their people, if given *sadaqah* and their counsel sought in *jihad* and other matters could lead them to become strong in their Islam. A case in point is that of the Makkans who became Muslims after the conquest of Makkah. The Prophet, upon whom be peace, gave them a large booty after his victory over the Huwazin. Most of them became very good and conscientious Muslims later on.

(3) Muslim residents at the borders: Muslims who live at the frontiers, close to enemy land, can also be given *sadaqah* as an incentive to defend the Islamic territory. The author of *al-Manar* claims that this falls under the national defense. Jurists place it under the share allocated for the cause of Allah. It is similar to a military expedition. In our times, people who most deserve our help are those Muslims whom the unbelievers have brought over to their side by placing them under their protection or converting such Muslims to their religion. We notice that colonial powers are working for the subjugation of all Muslims and are trying to divert them away from their religion. Such states are allocating a certain portion of their resources to win over the Muslim hearts. Some they have succeeded converting to Christianity, and others have been influenced by or attracted to their tutelage. This is creating problems for Muslim states and Islamic unity. Are not such Muslims more deserving of *zakah* than those along the frontiers?

(4) The *zakah* employees: Muslims who are employed to collect *zakah*, either through persuasion or force, from those who are not willing to give it can also qualify as its recipients for it is better to use such people to maintain Muslim unity. Their support and their undertaking to help the government is the lesser of two evils and a preferable arrangement.

The unbelievers: As for the unbelievers, they are of two categories:

(1) Those who may come to Islam through the reconciliation of their hearts: Such was the case of Safwan ibn 'Umayyah whom the Prophet, upon whom be peace, granted safety on the day of Makkah's conquest. The Prophet, upon whom be peace, allowed him to think about his situation for four months and then choose for himself. He was absent at the time but came forward later and went with the Muslims to fight in the battle of Hunayn before his acceptance of Islam. The Prophet, upon whom be peace, borrowed his armory for the expedition of Hunayn, and in return gave him a large number of camels, loaded with goods, that were at a certain valley. Thereupon Safwwan said: "This is a gift from someone who does not fear poverty. By Allah," he continued, "the Prophet, upon whom be peace, has given all of this to me and verily he is the person whom I dislike the most, but he continued to give me things until he became the one I loved the most."

(2) People whose evil is feared, and it is hoped that money, if given to them, will neutralize their hostility: Ibn 'Abbas reported: "A group of people used to come to the Prophet, upon whom be peace. If he gave them money, they would praise Islam and say: 'This is a good religion.' However, if he did not give them any money, they criticized and found fault with Islam." Among such people were Abu Sufyan ibn Harb, al-Aqra' ibn Habis, and 'Uyainah ibn Hisn. The Prophet, upon whom be peace, gave every one of them one hundred camels.

The Hanafiyyah say that the share of such people are cancelled when Islam is strong. For instance, 'Uyainah ibn Hisn, al-Aqra' ibn Habis, and al-'Abbas ibn Mirdas came to Abu Bakr and requested their share. He wrote them a letter, which they took to 'Umar. He tore the letter and said: "This is something that the Prophet, upon whom be peace, used to give you to reconcile you to Islam. Now, Allah has fortified Islam and it is no longer in need of you. Unless you stay with Islam, the sword will be between you and us. Say: 'It is the truth from the Lord of you [all]. Then whoever will, let him believe, and whoever will, let him disbelieve' [*al-Kahf*: 29]." They returned to Abu Bakr and said: "Are you the Caliph or is 'Umar? You wrote a letter for us and 'Umar tore it up." He answered: "This is the way it is."

The Hanafiyyah continue: "Indeed, Abu Bakr agreed with 'Umar, and none of the companions disapproved of it. Likewise, it was never reported from 'Uthman or 'Ali that they gave anything to anyone in this category."

It can be answered that the case under reference was 'Umar's own judgment. He saw that there would be no benefit in mollifying these people after Islam had become well-established among their people, and no harm would follow if they abandoned Islam. Also, if 'Uthman and 'Ali stopped spending this kind of endowment, this does not necessarily mean that the provision for it was repealed. It is possible that the change of circumstances did not call for the continuation of such an endowment to the nonbelievers. However, this does not amount to the invalidation of the provision for such endowments. Should the contingency call for its revival, the endowments in this category can be given. This is because their sanction lies in the Qur'an and *sunnah*.

Ahmad and Muslim reported from Anas that whenever the Prophet, upon whom be peace, was asked for anything for the sake of Islam, he would give it away. A man came and asked for *sadaqah*. The Prophet ordered that the man be given the entire lot of sheep between two mountains. These sheep were part of the *sadaqah*. The man returned to his people and said: "Oh my people! Accept Islam, for indeed, Muhammad gives in such a way as if he does not fear poverty." Ash-Shaukani says that al-'Itrah, al-Jobbani, al-Balkhi, and Ibn Mubashshir held that *sadaqah* may be given to those whose hearts are to be reconciled to Islam. On the contrary, ash-Shaf'i maintains that such endowments are not for unbelievers. As for the sinner (*fāsiq*), he may be given from such allocations.

Abu Hanifah and his followers hold that this kind of endowment was cancelled with the spread and domination of Islam and, as evidence, they cite Abu Bakr's refusal to restore endowments to Abu Sufyan, 'Uyainah, al-Aqra', and al-'Abbas ibn Mirdas. It appears that reconciliation is permitted when the need for it arises. In other words, it is permitted to give them *sadaqah* for reconciliation when a people obey a leader only for worldly affairs, and they cannot be controlled except by force and domination. The spread of Islam has no ramification on the issue of reconciliation because it makes no difference in this case. The author of *al-Manar* testifies: "This is the whole truth. Only independent judgment can be exercised to elaborate on the eligibility and the amount of *sadaqah* or booty to be given away when they are available, along with other kinds of property [immovable and movable]. It is necessary to seek consultation of capable people (*ahl ash-Shura*) as the caliphs did in those matters that required *ijtihad*. Whether a leader can force them into obedience by coercive action before resorting to the use of the endowment is an unsettled issue. Nevertheless, this cannot be followed as a rule but rather as the principle of inclining to the lesser of two evils and to the best benefit of the society."

V. Freeing Captives: This category includes two kinds of slaves: contracted slaves (*mukātabūn*) and regular slaves. Both categories were aided with *sadaqah* to obtain their freedom. Al-Bara' reported: "A man came to the Prophet, upon whom be peace, and said to him: 'Guide me to a deed that makes me close to Heaven and far from Hell.' The Prophet, upon whom be peace, said: 'Free a person and redeem a slave.'" Then al-Bara' asked: "O Messenger of Allah. Are not the two the same?" He answered: "No. Freeing a person is to grant him freedom [by redeeming him from his bondage], but the redeeming of the neck means buying him his freedom." This is related by Ahmad and ad-Daraqutni and their report is trustworthy.

Abu Hurairah reported that the Prophet, upon whom be peace, said: "Three persons have the right to be helped by Allah: the warrior (*ghazi*) who fights for Allah, the contracted slave who longs to buy his freedom, and one who wishes to get married for the sake of chastity." This is related by Ahmad and the *ashab as-Sunan*. At-Tirmidhi grades this report as good and sound.

As to the meaning of *free captives* (*wā fi ar-riqāb*), ash-Shaukani says that scholars differ over it. 'Ali ibn Abu Talib, Sa'id ibn Jubair, al-Layth, ath-Thauri, al-'Itrah, the Hanafiyyah, the Shaf'iyyah, and the majority of scholars are reported to believe that it refers to contracted slaves (*mukātabūn*) whose freedom is secured through payment from *zakah*. According to Ibn 'Abbas, al-Hasan al-Basri, Malik, Ahmad ibn Hanbal, Abu Thaur, and Abu 'Ubaid, it means using *zakah* in the release of any kind of slave. Al-Bukhari and Ibn al-Mundhir are also supportive of this view. Their rationale is that the expression *wā fi ar-riqāb* cannot be confined to the kind of slavery arising from a contract because, if that had been the case, then it would have fallen under the category of those in debt (*gharimīn*), for theirs is an obvious case of debt. As such, freeing a slave from bondage is better than helping a contracted slave. He could be aided or helped, but not freed, for the contracted slave is a slave as long as he owes even one *dirham*. At the same time, freeing a slave is possible at any time, in contrast to the situation of a contracted slave.

Commenting on the subject, az-Zuhri says that the preceding position entails two possibilities. The Qur'anic *'ayah* on the subject alludes to these two possibilities, which have been pointed out by ash-

Shaukani in his *Muntaqa al-Akhbar*. In the *hadith* narrated by al-Bara', evidence suggests that redeeming necks is not the same as freeing them. Nor is the deed of freeing slaves the same as helping contracted ones with money to pay off the contract. Both of these bring the individual closer to Heaven and distance him from Hell.

VI. Debtors: People burdened by debts and unable to pay them are of several kinds: those who took upon themselves responsibility to discharge a debt; those who guaranteed debts of others and therefore, upon default, the debts have become their obligation; those who mismanaged their finances, those who borrowed money because they had to; or those who were involved in sinful acts and then repented, and who had to pay a fine for repentance. All of them may take *sadaqah* to meet their debts.

Anas reported that the Prophet, upon whom be peace, said: "Asking for *sadaqah* is permissible only for the following three classes [of people]: (a) those who are in abject poverty, (b) those who have severe debts, or (c) those who incurred it in the payment of blood money [on behalf of a relative or friend]." This is related by Ahmad, Abu Dawud, Ibn Majah, and at-Tirmidhi. The latter grades it *hasn.*

Muslim relates from Abu Sa'id al-Khudri that a man made a bad deal on fruit and then ran into heavy debt. The Prophet, upon whom be peace, recommended: "Give him *sadaqah.*" Then the people gave him *sadaqah.* However, he still had some debt left over. Thereupon, the Prophet, upon whom be peace, said to creditors: "Take what you get ..."

As to the previously stated *hadith* of Qabisah ibn Mukhariq, in which he says: "I had a debt. I went to the Messenger of Allah, upon whom be peace, and asked him for help. He answered: 'Wait until we have received funds for *sadaqah*, then we will give some to you.' " The expression *hamalah* in this *hadith*, as defined by the scholars, is to assume someone's responsibility as one's own in order to restitute a discord. In pre-Islamic times, whenever strife took place among the Arab tribes and blood was spilled, compensation was called for. In such a case, one of them would volunteer to meet the obligation until the strife had ended. Undoubtedly, this was a noble act for these people. When the Arabs would come to know that one of them had taken upon himself the responsibility (*hamalah*) of someone's debt, they would hasten to his help in the discharge of his responsibility. If such a person asked for help, it was considered an honorable act and not derogatory to his character. No conditions were stipulated. As for being qualified to obtain *zakah* in the discharge of such debts, it is not a precondition that the person who has assumed the debt on another's behalf should be unable to pay it. In fact, he can still ask for *zakah* even though he is a man of means.

VII. Sadaqah for the Cause of Allah: *Fī sabīl lillāh* means *for the sake of Allah* — that is, making use of knowledge and deeds to attain Allah's pleasure. Most scholars understood this phrase as fighting for the cause of Allah. Part of *zakah* designated for the cause of Allah is given to volunteer fighters, especially those who are not on the payroll of the state, regardless of their financial status.

The *hadith* of the Messenger of Allah, stated elsewhere, also confirms it: "*Sadaqah* is not permitted to the rich except to the following five: the warrior (*ghazi*) for the cause of Allah ... and so on."

As to the pilgrimage (*hajj*), it does not fall under the *zakah* designated for the cause of Allah because it is an obligation for one who can afford it. Commenting on the issue, the authors of *al-Manar* say: "Spending of this portion on securing the routes of the pilgrimage and for providing water, food, and health services for the pilgrims is permissible if funds from other sources are not available."

Included in the share designated "for the cause of Allah" are those spendings in the interest of the common good that pertain to both religious and secular matters. The foremost is the preparations for war, including buying arms, food supplies for soldiers, means of transportation, and equipment for warriors. However, the supplies for warriors are to be returned to the treasury after the war. This applies especially to unconsumable items such as weapons, horses, and so on. A warrior does not always possess such items, for he uses them in the cause of Allah only when necessary. This is not the case, however, with other recipients of *zakah*, such as *zakah* collectors, debtors, people who received money under the expense account "reconciliation of hearts," and the wayfarers. They do not have to return the *zakah*, even if they are no longer entitled to it.

Also included in the expense account "for the cause of Allah" are projects such as establishing military hospitals, paved and unpaved roads, the extension of military (not commercial) railway lines, and the building of cruisers, warplanes, fortresses, and trenches. An important item in this category could be the preparation of Muslim missionaries and sending them to non-Muslim countries to spread Islam, just as non-Muslim missionaries are now spreading their religions in Islamic countries. Also falling under this heading would be school expenses to prepare adequate courses in religious sciences and in other areas of public interest. Teachers involved in such programs should be given *sadaqah* as long as they continue to perform their assigned jobs without resorting to other means of income. Scholars who are rich should not be paid for their work, despite their obvious benefits to the people.

VIII. Sadaqah for the Wayfarer: Scholars agree that a traveler stranded in a foreign land should be given *zakah* if he lacks the means to achieve his objectives. The extension of *zakah* is, however, tied to the condition that the journey must have been undertaken for Islamically acceptable reasons. Just what such a trip involves is open to question. The preferable opinion among the Shaf'iyyah is that *sadaqah* is given even when the traveler is taking the trip for sightseeing and pleasure. The wayfarer (*ibn as-sabil*), according to the Shaf'iyyah, is of two kinds: (1) a person traveling within his own country, and (2) one traveling in a foreign country. Both of them are entitled to *zakah*, even though they could find someone to lend them the needed amount and they have enough resources in their own country to pay their debts. According to Malik and Ahmad, only the passer-by is eligible for *zakah* and not one traveling within his own country. *Zakah* is not to be given to the person if he can find someone to lend him the money he needs and if he has enough of his own money in his country to pay his debt.

Who Has Priority?

The distribution of *zakah* to those who are eligible, as mentioned in the *'ayah* from *at-Taubah*, can now be classified as under:

The poor (*fuqūrā'*); the needy (*masākīn*); the administrators of *zakah* (*'amilūna 'alaihā*); those whose hearts are to be won over (*mu'allafatu qulubuhum*), slaves (*ar-riqab*); those in debt (*gharīmūn*) the wayfarers (*abna' as-Sabil*); the warriors (*mujāhidīn*).

The jurists differ over the distribution of *zakah* among the preceding eight groups of people.

Ash-Shaf'i and his followers hold that if a distributor of *zakah* happens to be the owner of the property (or the agent), then there is no share of the collectors in it. In that case, it becomes obligatory to distribute the sum collected among the remaining seven categories. If other categories are for some reason ineligible for their share, it will be distributed among those still eligible. It is not permissible to disregard any category if it meets the conditions for eligibility. Ibrahim an-Nakha'i says that if the amount of *zakah* received is large, then it is possible to divide it among the different categories. However, if it is small, it is permissible to place it into one category. Ahmad ibn Hanbal holds that the division of *zakah* has a priority but that it is permissible to give it all to one category. Malik maintains that the distributor of *zakah* should make an effort to investigate those who are in need. He should distribute it according to the immediate condition of the needy and poor people. Thus, if he sees in certain years that the poor need more, they should be given priority. If he sees in another year that the wayfarers are more needy, he should distribute it among the travelers. The Hanafiyyah and Sufyan ath-Thauri thought that the *zakah* payer can choose the categories he wished to distribute the *zakah* to. This is related by Hudhaifah and Ibn 'Abbas. Al-Hasan al-Basri and 'Ata' ibn Abi Rabah base their opinions on it. Abu Hanifah holds that the distributors of *zakah* may give it to one person under any of the eight categories.

Why the Scholars Differ

According to Ibn Rushd: "The cause of their differences lies between the literal and the intended meaning. The literal meaning determines the classifications, but the intended meaning shows that priority should be given to the needy according to the immediacy of their needs since the aim [of the institution of *zakah*] is to eliminate poverty. The enumeration [of the categories] in the Qur'an is meant to distinguish the different kinds — that is, the people eligible for *zakah*, and not necessarily their grouping. The first interpretation is the literal one while the second is the intended interpretation." Ash-Shaf'i builds his case on the *hadith* of as-Suda'i which is related by Abu Dawud. A man came to the Prophet, upon whom be peace, and asked for *zakah*. The Messenger of Allah, upon whom be peace, said: "Allah has not left the matter to the judgment of a prophet nor to others. He has laid the rules for it — that is, He has classified [the beneficiaries] into eight categories. If you fit into any of these, I will give you your due."

The Preference of the Majority's Opinion Over That of ash-Shaf'i

The author of *ar-Rawdah an-Nadiyyah* says: "Distributing all of the *zakah* to one group is more benefiting to the realization of the word of Allah." In brief, one may say that Allah made *zakah* applicable only to the eight specifically mentioned categories. Spelling out these categories does not mean that the *zakah* has to be distributed among them equally or even that it has to be divided among them. The intended meaning, however, is that the categories of *sadaqah* are similar to various groups of people who are eligible for it. Thus, one who is obligated to pay anything to any category of *sadaqah* and gives it to a person in a parallel group is considered to be fulfilling what Allah commanded him to do. Contrary to this, if one divides his *zakah* due into the acknowledged eight categories, if all eight exist, then that would not only be contrary to the practice of the Muslims throughout history, but it would cause hardship to the payer of *zakah*. For example, if the collected *zakah* were meager, it would be of no benefit to any designated category — even if it was of one kind, to say nothing if it was of numerous kinds. To endorse such a practice would be tantamount to counter what the Prophet, upon whom be peace, did when he permitted the payment of a penance (*kaffarah*) from the charity collected for Salmah ibn Sakhr. Obviously, the *hadith* of as-Suda'i cannot be used as evidence.

There is not a single case in the entire corpus of *hadith* literature which could be used to make the distribution of *zakah* to all groups of people obligatory. Using the *hadith* of Mu'adh as evidence that the Prophet, upon whom be peace, instructed him to take *zakah* from the rich Yemenites and give it to their poor will not be of much help because it does not establish that the *zakah* was distributed to all the groups. Nor is the *hadith* of Ziyad ibn al-Harith as-Suda'i valid in this regard because in its chain of narrators is 'Abdur-Rahman ibn Ziyad al-'Afriqi, whose credibility has been questioned by many scholars. Assuming that this *hadith* is valid for the point under discussion, the meaning of the division of *zakah* into parts is its distribution according to the apparent meaning of the Qur'anic *'ayah* and what the Prophet, upon whom be peace, had in mind. Assuming that the division of *zakah* itself is intended, the distribution has to be done according to the specified categories. In this case, any transfer of the share of one group to another, even if the group concerned was for some reason non-existent, will not be permissible. Such an approach will be contrary to the consensus of Muslim scholars. If we accept that, then the deciding factor for the *sadaqah*'s distribution is the leader's wish rather than, and not the specific categories of eligible people. Thus, there is no evidence that makes division obligatory, and it is consequently permissible to give some *sadaqah* to those eligible people and some to other groups. Indeed, when the leader collects all the *sadaqat* from his people and all eight categories are eligible to receive them, each group has the right to claim its share. However, he does not have to divide the collected *sadaqāt* among them equally or distribute it without any distinction, for he can give any amount to any group or groups that he wants to, or he can give some without giving the rest if he thinks it is in the interest of Islam and its people. For example, if the *sadaqah* was collected and then a *jihad* was announced, meaning that it would become necessary to defend the territory of Islam against the unbelievers, the leader can give some or all of it to the deserving warriors. This also applies to other concerns if the interest of Islam necessitates it.

People Forbidden for *Zakah*

We have discussed so far the distribution of *zakah* and the categories of people eligible to receive it. Now we will talk about those who are forbidden to receive it. They are:

I. Unbelievers and Atheists: The jurists agree that unbelievers and atheists are not to be given *zakah*. In the *hadith* which says: "*Zakah* is taken from the rich and given back to the poor," "the rich" refers to rich Muslims while "the poor" indicates poor Muslims. Ibn al-Mundhir said that all scholars agree that the free non-Muslim subject (**dhimmi**) is not entitled to *zakah*. Exceptions to the rule are those people whose hearts are leaning toward Islam. However, it is permissible to give a *dhimmi* from the nonobligatory charity (*tatawwu'*). Alluding to the characteristics of the belivers, the Qur'an says: "And for His love, they feed the indigent, orphan, and captive" (*ad-Dahr*: 8). This is also supported by the following *hadith*: "Be kind to your mother." The woman in this case was an unbeliever.

II. Banu Hashim: This includes the families of 'Ali, Ja'far, al-'Abbas, and al-Harith. Ibn Qudamah says there are no two opinions on the ineligibility of Banu Hashim to receive *zakah*. The Prophet, upon whom be peace, declared: "Indeed, *sadaqah* ought not to be given to the family of Muhammad ..." Muslim related it. Abu Hurairah reported that when al-Hasan took one date from the *sadaqah* dates, the Prophet, upon whom be peace, said to him: "Nay, spit it out! Don't you know that we cannot eat from charity?" Scholars agree on the authenticity of this *hadith*. As to the eligibility of Banu al-Muttalib for *zakah*, the scholars differ.

Ash-Shaf'i holds that like Banu Hashim they are disallowed to take *zakah*. Ash-Shaf'i, Ahmad, and al-Bukhari relate from Jubair ibn Mut'im who said: "At the battle of Khaibar, the Prophet, upon whom be peace, set aside the share of the relatives of the families of Banu Hashim and Banu al-Muttalib and left out the shares of Banu Nawfal and Banu 'Abd Shams. I and 'Uthman ibn 'Affan came to the Messenger of Allah, upon whom be peace, and said to him: 'O Messenger of Allah! Do not deny Banu Hashim the grace of their position because Allah placed you among them. How about our brothers Banu al-Muttalib? You gave them and left us out? Isn't our relationship one and the same?' The Prophet, upon whom be peace, answered: 'I and Banu al-Muttalib are not to be separated either during *jahiliyyah* or Islam. We and they are one.' Then he joined his fingers [in demonstrating the close relationship]." Reason dictates that one should not differentiate between them (the two families) in any matter of law because they are one according to the saying of the Prophet. It is evident that they are the family of Muhammad, and therefore, *sadaqāt* are forbidden to them. Abu Hanifah holds that the family of Banu al-Muttalib may take from *zakah*. Both these reports are related by Ahmad. Just as the Messenger of Allah, upon whom be peace, made charity unlawful for the family of Banu Hashim, he also made it unlawful for their proteges (*mawla*). Abu Rafi', a protege of the Prophet, said that the latter appointed a man from the family of Banu Makhzum to collect *sadaqat*. This man said to Abu Rafi': "Accompany me so that you may get some of it." He said: "No, until I meet the Messenger of Allah, upon whom be peace, and ask him." He left and asked him. The Prophet answered: "*Sadaqah* is not lawful for us — and the proteges of a certain tribe are like [the members of the tribe] themselves." Ahmad, Abu Dawud, and at-Tirmidhi related it. The latter grades it good (*hassan*) and sound (*sahih*).

Whether nonobligatory charity (*tatawwu'*) is lawful for the family of the Prophet or not, scholars differ. Ash-Shaukani, having summarized the views on the issue, says: "The apparent meaning of the Prophet's *hadith*, '*Sadaqah* is unlawful for us,' is the unlawfulness of the obligatory as well as nonobligatory *sadaqat*." A group of scholars, including al-Khattabi, says that its prohibition for the Prophet, upon whom be peace, carries consensus. Based on ash-Shaf'i's report, many others have ruled that the prohibition of *zakah* to the Prophet does not include the nonobligatory charity. A report from Ahmad equally says so but Ibn Qudamah rejects all these reports for lack of clear evidence.

As for the family of the Prophet, upon whom be peace, the vast majority of the Hanafiyyah, the Shaf'iyyah, the Hanbaliyyah, and the majority of the Zaidiyyah hold that nonobligatory *sadaqah* is permissible for them but not the obligatory one, since to them the latter is nothing but filth that comes out from people's holdings. This is understood to mean that the (prescribed) *zakah* and not the nonobligatory *sadaqat*, are forbidden to them. It is said in *al-Bahr* that nonobligatory *sadaqah* is restricted by being confined to a donation, gift, or endowment. Abu Yusuf and Abu al-'Abbas maintain that it is unlawful for them, as is the prescribed charity, because there is no evidence of the contrary.

III. Fathers and Sons: The jurists agree that it is not permissible to give *zakah* to one's father, grandfather, mother, grandmother, son, grandson, daughter, and her children because the *zakah* payer is obligated to take care of all such people anyway. In case of their poverty, they should draw upon his largesse because it is their right. Thus, if he pays them *zakah*, he benefits himself and avoids the obligation of supporting them. Malik exempts the grandfather, grandmother, grandsons, and granddaughters because one does not have an obligation to support them if they are poor. However, if they are well-off and fought voluntarily for the cause of Allah, the *zakah* payer may give them some of the *zakah* designated for those fighting in the cause of Allah. He may also give them some of the share meant for debtors, though he is not obligated to pay off their debts. He may also give them a portion of the amount set aside for *zakah* collectors, provided they are in this category.

IV: The Wife: Ibn al-Mundhir says that all scholars agree that a man is not obligated to give his wife *zakah*, the reason being that adequate support for her is already enjoined upon him, unless she is in debt. In that case, she may be given from the debtor's share to pay off her debt.

V. The Distribution of *Zakah* in Order to Grow Nearer to Allah: It is not permissible to distribute *zakah* so as to grow nearer to Allah other than what Allah, the Exalted One, mentions in the *'ayah*: "The alms are only for the poor and the needy" (*at-Taubah*: 60). Thus, *zakah* cannot be paid for establishing mosques, bridges, road repair, hospitality, shrouding the dead, and so on. Abu Dawud witnesses: "I heard Ahmad while he was asked whether spending part of the *zakah* on shrouding the deceased was permissible. He said: 'No. Nor can it be used to pay the debt of the dead.'" He also said: "One can pay the debt of a living person from the *zakah* but not that of the deceased. For a person who dies, there is no debt."

Ahmad was also asked what would happen if it had been given to help them redeem their debt. He answered: "Yes, for his family it is all right."

Who Distributes *Zakah*?

The Messenger of Allah used to send his authorized agents to collect *zakah*. He would then distribute it among the deserving people. Abu Bakr and 'Umar did the same. There is no difference between unhidden wealth (i.e., plants, fruit, cattle, and minerals) and hidden wealth (i.e., trade goods, gold, silver, and treasure). When 'Uthman became caliph, he followed this practice for a while. Later on, when he saw that the hidden wealth was tremendous and that pursuing it embarrassed the community and while checking it harmed its owners, he left the payment of the *zakah* on such property to the individual's discretion. Jurists agree that the owners themselves should assume the distribution of *zakah*, especially when it is for hidden wealth. As-Sa'ib ibn Yazid reported: "I once heard the Messenger of Allah, upon whom be peace. He said: 'This is the month of your *zakah*. If any one of you still owes a debt, let him pay it off so that your properties become free from debts. Then, you can pay the *zakah* on them.'" Al-Baihaqi relates it with a *sahih* chain.

An-Nawawi says that some scholars agree with this practice.

Is it preferable for the owners to distribute the *zakah* due on their hidden wealth, or is it preferable to let the leader distribute it?

There is more than one opinion on this subject. The preferred choice among the Shaf'iyyah is that *zakah* be paid to the government, especially when it is a just government. According to the Hanbaliyyah, it is preferable that the *zakah* payer distribute it himself, even though it is permissible to give it to the ruler. On the other hand, Malik and the Hanafiyyah hold that if the wealth is unhidden, the Muslim leader and his agents have the authority to ask for and take their *zakah*. The opinion of the Shaf'iyyah and the Hanbaliyyah concerning unhidden wealth is similar to that on the hidden ones.

Paying *Zakah* to the Leader, Regardless of His Being Just or Unjust

It is permissible to pay *zakah* to a Muslim leader, whether he is just or not, provided he rules (more or less) according to Islamic laws. The property owner absolves himself of his obligation by giving *zakah* to the leader. If the leader does not distribute it properly, it is preferable that the property owner do so himself, unless the leader or his agent asks for it.

Anas reported: "A man from the tribe of Banu Tamim came to the Messenger of Allah, upon whom be peace, and said: 'O Messenger of Allah! If I paid the *zakah* to your representative, am I acquitted of my responsibility?' The Messenger of Allah, upon whom be peace, said: 'Yes, if you pay it to my representative, then you have acquitted yourself. Its reward will be yours and its sin will be upon whoever misused it.'" This is related by Ahmad.

Ibn Mas'ud reported that the Prophet, upon whom be peace, said: "After me, there will be selfishness and you will deny obligations." They said: "O Messenger of Allah! What do you command us to do?" He answered: "Pay the due which is upon you and ask Allah what is right for you." This is related by al-Bukhari and Muslim.

Wa'il ibn Hajar reported: "I heard the Messenger of Allah, upon whom be peace, say after a man had asked him his opinion of our leaders who deny their right [of collecting and distributing the *zakah*]: 'Listen and obey, for indeed, they have their responsibility and you have yours.'" This is related by Muslim.

Commenting on the subject, ash-Shaukkani says that the *'ahadith* cited in this section are used by many scholars to justify the permissibility of transferring both kinds of *zakah* to unjust rulers. This applies to rulers of Muslims in the world of Islam (*Dar al-Islam*).

As to contemporary Muslim governments, Sheikh Rashid Rida says: "At present, the majority of Muslims do not have an Islamic government which establishes Islam, propagates and defends it, calls for *jihad* individually or collectively, implements its divine injunctions, and collects and distributes *zakah* according to the rules laid down by Allah, the Exalted One.

Some of the Muslim rulers are under the influence of Western powers, while others are under the tutelage of polytheists. These foreign powers employ Muslim leaders as tools to subjugate the people in the name of Islam, thus destroying Islam itself. They use the influence of the Muslim leaders and Muslim resources, including *zakah* and endowments, to further their interests. To such rulers, it is not permissible to pay any part of *zakah*, regardless of their title or profession of faith. As for the rest of the Islamic governments whose rulers and heads of state profess Islam and whose finances are not controlled by foreigners, the payment of unhidden *zakah* should be made to their leaders. This also applies to hidden properties, such as gold and silver, when the leaders request it, even if they are unjust in some of their judgments, as is said by the jurists."

The Preferability of Giving *Zakah* to Good People

Zakah is given to a Muslim provided he is eligible to receive it. Whether he is good or sinful does not matter. If, however, it is known that he will use it to perpetuate what Allah has forbidden, it should be denied to him. It is preferable that one who pays *zakah* should give it to the pious, the knowledgeable, and those of kind disposition. It is related from Abu Sa'id al-Khudri that the Prophet, upon whom be peace, said: "The likeness of a believer and the likeness of belief are similar to the horse that, tied to its post, walks around and then comes back to its post. The believer may forget, but he returns to his belief. Thus, give your food to the righteous people and entrust your favors to the believers." This is related by Ahmad with a good chain and as-Suyuti authenticated it.

Ibn Taimiyyah says that the needy who discards his *salah* will not be given anything until he repents and offers *salah* again because neglecting *salah* is a grave sin. It is not right that one who commits this sin should be financially helped until he repents to Allah. Included along with those who neglect *salah* are offenders who are not ashamed to commit sinful acts and remain unrepentant. Also, one whose conscience is corrupted has an innate character which is distorted and a sense of good which is virtually dead. Such a person is not given *zakah* unless doing so will turn him in the right direction and help him reform.

The *Zakah* Giver is Forbidden to Buy Back What He Gave in Charity

The Messenger of Allah, upon whom be peace, prohibited the one who gives *zakah* to buy back what he gave up for Allah, the Exalted One. This is similar to the case of those immigrants who were prohibited (by the Messenger) to return to Makkah after they had left it as immigrants. It is related by 'Abdullah ibn 'Umar that: "Once 'Umar gave away a horse, for the cause of Allah, as *sadaqah*. Later, he saw it for sale and wanted to buy it. He asked the Messenger of Allah, upon whom be peace, if he could do so. The Messenger answered: 'Do not buy back what you gave in *sadaqah*.'" This is related by al-Bukhari, Muslim, Abu Dawud, and an-Nasa'i. An-

Nawawi says it is a purifying prohibition, not one of unlawfulness. It is unsuitable (*makruh*) for a person to buy back what he has given in *sadaqah*, or *zakah*, or penance for a promise, or anything of the nature which brings one closer to Allah, the Exalted One. This is also applicable to a gift offered to someone which the donor cannot own even if it is allowed by the recipient. However, it can be owned by him again if he inherits it. According to Ibn Battal, most scholars disliked someone to buy his *sadaqah* back. This is in accordance with 'Umar's *hadith*. Ibn al-Mundhir says that al-Hasan, 'Ikrimah, Rabi'ah, and al-Auza'i allowed buying one's charity back. Ibn Hazm is also inclined to this view because of a *hadith* from Abu Sa'id al-Khudri. The Messenger of Allah, upon whom be peace, said: "*Sadaqah* is not allowed to the well-to-do except for five among them: one who fights in the cause of Allah; one who administers *zakah*; one who is in debt; one who bought [the article of *zakah*] with his money; or one who has a poor neighbor to whom he gave *sadaqah*, and the latter gave it as a gift to him."

Preference in Giving *Zakah* to Husband or Relatives

A poor husband is entitled to receive *zakah* from his well-to-do wife, even though she is not supposed to support him. Her reward for giving it to him is more than if she were to give it to strangers. Abu Sa'id al-Khudri reported that Zainab, the wife of Ibn Mas'ud, said: "O Prophet of Allah! Indeed you have ordered us today to give away *sadaqah*, and I have some jewelry which I wanted to give away as *sadaqah*. But Ibn Mas'ud claims that he and his children deserve it more than someone else." The Prophet, upon whom be peace, responded: "Ibn Mas'ud is right. Your husband and your children are more deserving." This is related by al-Bukhari. Ash-Shaf'i, Ibn al-Mundhir, Abu Yusuf, Muhammad, the Zahiriyyah, and one of the reports by Ahmad hold the same view. Abu Hanifah and other scholars differ, saying that the wife is not allowed to give any *sadaqah* to her husband. They maintain that Zainab's *hadith* is concerned with voluntary *sadaqah* and not with the obligatory one. Malik holds that it is not permissible for a husband to spend the *sadaqah* he receives from his wife on her. Spending it on others is all right. Most scholars say that one's brothers, sisters, paternal uncles and aunts, and maternal uncles and aunts may receive *zakah* if they are eligible. Their opinion is based on the *hadith* which says: "*Sadaqah* for the poor is rewarded as one *sadaqah*, but in the case of a relative it is considered as two: [one reward for] blood tie and [the other reward for] the *sadaqah* [itself]." This is related by Ahmad, an-Nasa'i, and at-Tirmidhi. The latter grades it *hassan*.

Giving Charity to Seekers of Religious Knowledge

An-Nawawi holds that if someone is able to earn a suitable living and wants to occupy himself by studying some of the religious sciences but finds that his work will not allow him to do so, then he may be given *zakah* since seeking knowledge is considered a collective duty (*fard kifayah*). As for the individual who is not seeking knowledge, *zakah* is not permissible for him if he is able to earn his living even though he resides at a school. An-Nawawi says: "As for one who is engaged in supererogatory worship (*nawafil*) or for one who occupies himself in *nawafil* with no time to pursue his own livelihood, he may not receive *zakah*. This is because the benefit of his worship is confined only to him, contrary to the one who seeks knowledge."

Setting Debt Free through *Zakah*

Formulating the issue, an-Nawawi says in *al-Majmū*: "Suppose a person owes a debt to another person and at the same time he qualifies for *zakah*. [When *zakah* is due for the lender to pay,] he tells [the borrower]: 'Consider the debt for [my] *zakah*.' Would it be valid?" An-Nawawi says there are two opinions on it. According to Ahmad and Abu Hanifah, who held the better opinion, it does not constitute *zakah* because it cannot be discharged unless actually paid, while Hasan al-Basri and 'Ata maintain that the responsibility to pay *zakah* will be discharged even though there is no payment of *zakah* (at that point in time) by its payer.

Likewise, if an individual trustingly assigns some money to a person to keep and at the time of *zakah* he asks the assignee to keep the amount in lieu of his *zakah*, it will be valid.

The jurists, however, agree that if a person pays *zakah* to another who owes him money and then receives it back to redeem his loan to him, the obligation to pay *zakah* will not be discharged. It is also invalid for a person to accept *zakah* on the condition that he will pay it back to the lender (the *zakah* payer) for the amount he owes him. Nevertheless, if at the time of lending and acceptance of the loan both agree to do so, even though it was not mentioned in the deal, it will be valid as *zakah*.

Transfer of *Zakah*

The jurists agree that *zakah* can be transferred from one city to another provided the needs of the city residents whom the *zakah* was originally derived from have first been satisfied. A large number of *ahadith* on the subject stress the need for depleting *zakah* among the poor and the needy of the city from which it is collected. This is because *zakah* aims at freeing the poor inhabitants of an area from want, and thus its transfer would contribute to their deprivation. This is substantiated by the *hadith* of Mu'adh: "Tell them that there is a charity due upon them to be taken from their rich and to be given back to their poor." Abu Juhaifah reported: "The charity collector of the Messenger of Allah, upon whom be peace, came to us and took *zakah* from our rich and gave it to our poor. I was an orphan then, and he gave me a young she-camel." This is related by at-Tirmidhi, who graded it *hassan*.

'Imran ibn Husain reports that he was employed as a charity collector. When he returned from this assignment, he was asked: "Where is the collection?" He responded: "Did you send me for the collection? We took it and distributed it the way we did at the time of the Messenger of Allah, upon whom be peace." This is related by Abu Dawud and Ibn Majah. On the same subject, Tawus says: "Mu'adh wrote in his letter: 'Anyone who moves from one location to another, his charity and tithe remain in the location of his tribe.'" This is related by al-Athram in his *Sunan*.

Based on such *ahadith*, the jurists say that the poor of a city have a prior claim over the local *zakah* than the poor elsewhere. Still, they differ over which conditions must prevail before *zakah* can be transferred from one city to another.

The Hanafiyyah hold that transferring *zakah* is disliked (*makruh*) unless it is for needy relatives and serves the ties of blood, or when the needs of a group of Muslims are more pressing than those of the locals, when it is tied to the general interests of the Muslims, when it is sought from a country at war against the Muslims to the land of Islam, when it is intended for a scholar, or when *zakah* is paid before the completion of the *hawl*. In those cases, transferring *zakah* is not disliked (*makruh*).

The Shaf'iyyah maintain that transferring *zakah* is not allowed and that it must be spent in the area of its origin, unless it has no poor or other categories of *zakah* recipients. 'Amr ibn Shu'aib reported that the Messenger of Allah, upon whom be peace, appointed Mu'adh ibn Jabal to a position in Jund where the latter remained until the death of the Prophet. At the time of this event, he came to 'Umar who reappointed him. He sent to 'Umar one-third of the *sadaqāt* collected from the local people, but 'Umar turned it down and said: "I did not appoint you to go there as a tax collector or as a tribute (*jizyah*) taker. I appointed you to collect *sadaqāt* from the rich and then to return them to their poor." Mu'adh replied: "I would not have sent you anything [from the collection] if I had found someone deserving [over here]."

In the second year, he sent him half of the collected *sadaqat*, and they ran into the same issue again. In the third year, he sent him all of it, and 'Umar again argued with him. Mu'adh responded: "I could not find anyone who deserved to receive anything from me." This is related by Abu 'Ubaid.

Malik holds that transferring *zakah* is allowed only when there is a desperate need. The administration then can send it to the other place after due consideration of all the facts. The Hanbaliyyah say that it is not permissible to transfer *zakah* from its place of origin to that of the place beyond which *salat ul-qasr* is applicable. It must be spent in the place which generated it or near to it but not beyond the point of *qasr*.

Abu Dawud says: "I heard Ahmad saying 'no' when asked if *zakah* could be transferred from one city to another. Asked further, 'What if his [the *zakah* payer's] relatives are in the other city?' he replied: 'No. It can be transferred only when the needs of the poor residents of a city have been satisfied.' " This is based on the preceding *hadith* of Abu 'Ubaid. Ibn Qudamah holds that even if the *zakah* payer violated the above stipulations by transferring it, he would still have met his obligation. Most of the scholars also support this view. When a man resides in one city and his holdings happen to be in another, consideration will be given to the city where his holdings are located because the holdings generated *zakah* and the eligible people will be eyeing it. If part of the holdings are with the owner and some are in another city, *zakah* will be paid on the portion in each city. This applies to *zakah* on one's holdings. As for the *zakah* at the end of Ramadan (*zakat ul-fitr*), it is distributed in the city where it is due, whether the payer's holdings are there or not. This is because this type of *zakah* is associated with the person rather than with the holdings.

Errors in the Distribution of *Zakah*

The topic of recipients versus non-recipients of *zakah* has already been covered. It does happen, however, that a *zakah* payer inadvertantly gives it to an ineligible person at the expense of an eligible one. Upon the realization of such a mistake, would he be considered to have fulfilled his obligation of *zakah* or would it still be a debt upon him until he pays it to the right people? The jurists differ over this point. Abu Hanifah, Muhammad, al-Hasan, and Abu 'Ubaidah maintain that in such a case he would not be required to pay another *zakah*.

Ma'an ibn Yazid reports: "My father set aside a few *dinars* for *sadaqah* and gave them to a man in the mosque. I went and took them and brought them back to my father. He said: 'By Allah! What have you done?' I consulted the Prophet, upon whom be peace, about it. The Prophet observed: 'O Yazid, for you is what you intended and O Ma'an, for you is what you have taken.' " This is related by Ahmad and al-Bukhari. The meaning of this *hadith* is that *sadaqah* is supererogatory (*nafl*); however, the word *ma* (meaning what) in *laka ma nawayta* (for you is what you intended) denotes generalization. Abu Hanifah and Muhammad are supported in their stand by a *hadith* from Abu Hurairah which reports the Prophet, upon whom be peace, saying: "A man [from Banu Isra'il] said [to himself]: 'Tonight I will give away something in *sadaqah*.' So he went out with his *sadaqah* and [unknowlingly] gave it to a thief. The next morning he was told by the people that he had given *sadaqah* to a thief. [On hearing this,] he said: 'O Allah! Praised be You. Certainly I will give *sadaqah* again.' So, he went out with his *sadaqah* and [unknowingly] gave it to an adulteress. The next morning he was told that he had given *sadaqah* to an adulteress. The man said: 'O Allah! Praised be You. [I gave my *sadaqah*] to an adulteress. Certainly I will give *sadaqah* again.' Thus he went out with his *sadaqah* again and [unknowingly] gave it to a rich person. The next morning the people said that the night before he had given his *sadaqah* to a wealthy person. He said: 'O Allah! Praised be You. [I have given my *sadaqah*] to an adulteress, a thief, and a rich person.' [In his dreams] he saw someone saying to him: 'The *sadaqah* you gave to the thief might make him abstain from stealing, and that given to the adulteress might make her abstain from illegal sex [adultery], and that given to the wealthy person might make him learn a lesson from it and spend his wealth, which Allah,

the Exalted One, has given him in Allah's cause.' " This is related by
Ahmad, al-Bukhari, and Muslim.

The Prophet, upon whom be peace, said to a man who asked
him for *sadaqah*: "If you were eligible for *zakah*, I would have
given you your due." He (the Prophet) gave (*zakah*) to two well-
built persons saying: "If you wish, I will give from it [*sadaqah*].
There is no portion in it for a wealthy person or a healthy individual
who is earning." Ibn Qudamah says: "If he would have considered
the reality of the rich person, he would not have been contented
with what they said [concerning this matter]."

The opinion of Malik, ash-Shaf'i, Abu Yusuf, ath-Thauri, and
Ibn al-Mundhir is that it will not be sufficient for a *zakah* payer to
give it to the undeserving, especially when his mistake becomes
clear. In that case, he should pay *zakah* once again to those who
deserve it. His case is similar to the case of unpaid debts (owed) to
other people. Ahmad says that there are two opinions concerning
one paying *zakah* to a person whom he thought was poor and later
learned was rich. The first contends it would be considered paid,
while the second says that it would not be. When it becomes known
that one who received *zakah* is a slave, an unbeliever, a Hashimite
(a person from the Prophet's family), or an ineligible relative of the
zakah payer, then one has not discharged one's obligation, the reason being that it is difficult to know who is rich and who is poor:
"The ignorant man thinks that since they [who do not ask for] are
modest they are free from want" [*al-Baqarah*: 273].

Disclosure of *Sadaqah*

It is permissible for the person giving *sadaqah* to disclose his
sadaqah, whether it is of an obligatory or supererogatory type
(*nafilah*), so long as he does not do it ostentatiously. However, it is
preferable not to disclose it. Allah, the Exalted One, says: "If you
publicize your almsgiving, it is alright, but if you hide it and give it
to the poor, it will be better for you" [*al-Baqarah*: 271]. Ahmad, al-
Bukhari, and Muslim relate from Abu Hurairah that the Prophet,
upon whom be peace, said: "Seven people will be shaded by Allah on
the day when there will be no shade except His. These people are: a
just ruler, a young man who has been brought up in the worship of
Allah, a man whose heart is attached to the mosque, two persons
who love each other only for Allah's sake and they meet and depart
in Allah's cause only, a person who gives *sadaqah* so secretly that
his left hand does not know what his right hand has given, a person

who remembers Allah in his seclusion and his eyes get filled with tears, and a man who refuses the call of a charming woman of noble birth for illicit sex and says: 'I am afraid of Allah, the Exalted One.' "

ZAKAT UL-FITR

Zakat ul-fitr is a type of *sadaqah* which must be paid by every Muslim, young and old, male and female, free and slave, at the end of the month of fasting (Ramadan).

Al-Bukhari and Muslim relate from Ibn 'Umar that he said: "The Prophet, upon whom be peace, enjoined the payment of one *sa'l* of dates or one *sa'* of barley as *zakat ul-fitr* on every Muslim, young and old, male and female, free and slave."

The Purpose of *Zakat ul-Fitr*

Zakat ul-fitr was made obligatory in the month of Sha'ban in the second year of the *hijrah*. Its purpose is to purify one who fasts from any indecent act or speech and to help the poor and needy. This view is based upon the *hadith* reported by Abu Dawud, Ibn Majah, and ad-Daraqutni from Ibn 'Abbas. The Messenger of Allah, upon whom be peace, enjoined *zakat ul-fitr* on the one who fasts to shield one's self from any indecent act or speech and for the purpose of providing food for the needy. It is accepted as *zakah* for the person who pays it before the *'id salah*, and it is *sadaqah* for the one who pays it after the *salah*.

Who Must Pay *Zakat ul-Fitr*

Zakat ul-fitr is incumbent on every free Muslim who possesses one *sa'* of dates or barley which is not needed as a basic food for himself or his family for the duration of one day and night. Every free Muslim must pay *zakat ul-fitr* for himself, his wife, children, and servants.

The Amount of *Zakat ul-Fitr*

The required amount of *zakat ul-fitr* is one *sa'*[10] of wheat, barley, raisins, dry cottage cheese (*aqit*), rice, corn, or similar items considered as basic foods (*qut*). Abu Hanifah made it permissible to set aside, as a *zakat ul-fitr*, an equivalent value and also said that if the payer pays in wheat, one-half of a *sa'* would be sufficient. Abu Sa'id al-Khudri reported: "We used to give on behalf of every child, old person, freeman, and slave during the lifetime of the Messenger of Allah, upon whom be peace, one *sa'* of food, or one *sa'* of dried cottage cheese, or one *sa'* of barley, or one *sa'* of dates, or one *sa'* of raisins as *zakat ul-fitr*. We continued to do so until Mu'awiyyah came to us to perform pilgrimage (*hajj*) or a minor pilgrimage (*'umrah*). He then addressed the people from the pulpit and said to them: 'I see that two *mudds*[11] of wheat of Syria equals one *sa'* of dates.' The people accepted that." However, Abu Sa'id contended: "I would continue to give as I used to give, namely, one *sa'* as long as I live." This is related by most *hadith* narrators. At-Tirmidhi remarks: "Some of the scholars gave one *sa'* from every charitable item [which is accepted as a sound practice]." Ash-Shaf'i and Ishaq sustain this view but some other scholars gave one *sa'* from every charitable item except wheat, of which only half a *sa'* would be sufficient. This is the saying of Sufyan, Ibn al-Mubarak, and the scholars of Kufah.

When *Zakat ul-Fitr* is Due

The jurists agree that *zakat ul-fitr* is due at the end of Ramadan. They differ, however, about the exact time.

---

[10]One *sa'* equals approximately three kilograms.

[11]One *mudd* equals two-thirds of one kilogram.

Ath-Thauri, Ahmad, Ishaq, and ash-Shaf'i (in his later opinion), and Malik (in one of his reports) are of the opinion that it is due at the sunset of the night of breaking the fast, for this is when the fast of Ramadan ends. Abu Hanifah, al-Layth, ash-Shaf'i (in his original opinion), and the second report of Malik say that *zakat ul-fitr* is due at the start of *fajr* on the day of *'id*.

These two different views acquire relevance if a baby is born after sunset but before dawn on the day of *'id*; the question then is whether *zakat ul-fitr* is obligatory for the baby or not. In accordance with the first view, it is not since the birth took place after the prescribed time, while according to the second view, it is due because the birth took place within the prescribed space of time.

Paying *Zakat ul-Fitr* in Advance

Most scholars believe that it is permissible to pay *zakat ul-fitr* a day or two before *'id*. Ibn 'Umar reports that the Messenger, upon whom be peace, ordered them to pay *zakat ul-fitr* before the people went out to perform the *'id* prayers. Nafi' reports that 'Umar used to pay it a day or two before the end of Ramadan. However, scholars hold different opinions when a longer time period is involved. According to Abu Hanifah, it is permissible to pay it even before Ramadan. Ash-Shaf'i holds that it is permissible to do so at the beginning of Ramadan. Malik and Ahmad (in his well-known view) maintain that it is permissible to pay it only one or two days in advance.

The founders of the four accepted Islamic legal schools agree that *zakat ul-fitr* is not nullified simply by not paying it on its due date. If such is the case, it becomes a debt on the one responsible for it until it is paid. They also agree that it is not permissible to delay it until the day of *'id*, but Ibn Sirin and an-Nakha'i say that this can be done. Ahmad says: "I hope that there is no harm [in the delay of its payment]." Ibn Raslan says that there is a consensus that its payment cannot be delayed just because it is a type of *zakah*. Thus, any delay is a sin and is analogous to delaying one's prayers without an acceptable excuse. This is proved by the following *hadith*: "If one pays *zakat ul-fitr* before the *salah*, it is considered an accepted *zakah*. If he pays it after the *salah*, it is considered an ordinary *sadaqah*."

Distribution of *Zakat ul-Fitr*

The distribution of *zakat ul-fitr* is the same as that of *zakah* — that is, it has to be distributed to the eight groups of beneficiaries mentioned in the *'ayah*: "The alms are only for the poor ..." [*at-Taubah*: 60]. The category comprising the poor is considered the most deserving. This is also supported by the *hadith*: "The Messenger of Allah, upon whom be peace, enjoined *zakat ul-fitr* as a purification for the one who fasts from any indecent act or speech, and as food for the needy."

Al-Baihaqi and ad-Daraqutni relate from Ibn 'Umar who said: "The Messenger of Allah, upon whom be peace, enjoined the *zakat ul-fitr*, and also said: 'Free them from want on this day.' "

Giving *Zakat ul-Fitr* to a *Dhimmi*

Az-Zuhri, Abu Hanifah, Muhammad, and Ibn Shubrumah make it permissible to give *zakat ul-fitr* to a *dhimmi*. Allah, the Exalted One, says: "Allah allows you to show kindness and deal justly with those who did not war against you on account of religion and did not drive you out from your homes. Lo! Allah loves those who are just" [*al-Mumtahanah: 8*].

Are There Other Claims on Wealth Besides *Zakah*?

Islam views wealth realistically — as an essential aspect of life and the main means of subsistence of individuals and groups. Allah, the Exalted One, instructs: "Give not to those who are weak of understanding [what is in] your wealth which Allah has made a means of support for you" [*an-Nisa'*: 5]. This amounts to saying that wealth is to be distributed to meet the basic needs of food, clothing, lodging, and other indispensables, and that no one is to be lost, forgotten, or left without support. The best way to distribute wealth so that everyone's basic needs are met is through *zakah*. It does not place any burden on the wealthy yet at the same time it meets the basic needs of the poor and relieves them of the hardships of life and the pain of deprivation. *Zakah* is not a favor (*minnah*) that the wealthy bestow upon the poor; rather, it is a due (*haqq*) that Allah entrusted in the hands of the rich to deliver to the poor and distribute among the deserving. Thus, the eminent truth about wealth and property is established — that is, wealth is not exclusively for the rich but for both the rich and the poor. This becomes obvious because of Allah's judgment concerning the distribution of booty (*fay'*). Allah warns: ". . . that it does not become a commodity taken by turns among the rich of you" [*al-Hashr*: 7]. This means it is an apportionment of wealth between the rich and the poor, not something restricted to the wealthy. *Zakah* is an obligation due on the property of those able to pay and is to be used to meet the basic needs of the poor and the needy so that they could be kept away from hunger and they could be given a sense of security and general well-being. If the amount of *zakah* is not enough to alleviate the conditions of the poor and the needy, then the rich can be subjected to further taxation. How much should be taken is not specified. Its quantity will be determined by the needs of the poor.

In his interpretation of *al-Baqarah*: 177, al-Qurtubi says: "The saying of Allah, the Exalted One: 'And to spend of your wealth out of love for Him' gives credence to those who maintain that there is a due on wealth other than *zakah* known as *mal addir*." Others hold that the preceding *'ayah* alludes to the obligatory *zakah*. According to ad-Daraqutni's report from Fatimah bint Qais, the first view is more convincing. She relates: "Indeed, there is a due on one's holdings other than the prescribed *zakah*." Then he recited the following Qur'anic verse: "It is not righteousness that you turn your faces to the East or to the West, but it is to believe in Allah, the Last Day, the Angels, the Book, the Messengers, and to spend of your wealth out of love for Him on your kin, orphans, the needy, the wayfarer, or those who ask, and on the ransom of slaves . . ." [*al-Baqarah*: 177]. Ibn Majah mentioned it in his *Sunan* and at-Tirmidhi in his *Jami'*. The latter says that Ibn Majah's has a different chain of narrators than his. Besides, Abu Hamzah and Maymun al-'A'war consider Ibn Majah's chain of narrator not credible. This *hadith* is related by Bayan and Isma'il ibn Salim from ash-Shu'bi, who said that it is sound.

The latter says: "If there is a question about its authenticity, it is rendered clear by the context of the *'ayah* [*al-Baqarah*: 177]. In this statement: '. . . to be steadfast in prayer, and to give *zakah*,' Allah mentions *zakah* with *salah*, which substantiates the fact that 'to spend of your property out of love for Him' does not refer to obligatory *zakah*, for that would be redundant in the *'ayah* — and Allah knows best."

The scholars agree that should a need arise, even when *zakah* has been paid, the Muslim community is bound to contribute toward the alleviation of the problem.

Malik says: "It is obligatory for the people to ransom those taken as prisoners of war, even if doing so consumes all their property. The consensus on this subject strengthens our view, and we seek success only through Allah." According to al-Manar, the 'ayah "... and to spend your property out of love for Him ..." [al-Baqarah: 177] means that one should give the property for the sake of Allah or for the love of giving it.

Imam Muhammad 'Abduh's comments are: "The giving of property in excess of the due zakah is considered one of the basic elements of piety (birr) and is enjoined like the prescribed zakah."

Whenever the exigency calls for it, sadaqah other than zakah is given. That could be before the completion of the year (hawl) or after the payment of zakah. The contribution is not based on a specific amount of nisab but on the ability to give. Thus, if someone possesses only a loaf of bread and sees a person who is more hard-pressed than himself, he should give it to that person. The hard-pressed person is not the only one who has a right to be satisfied, but Allah has also ordered the believers to give non-prescribed sadaqat to the following:

Kin (dhawī al-Qūrbā): The kin are considered the most deserving people for the sadaqah gift because of the common blood relationship. When a man is in need and some of his relatives are rich, naturally he looks to them for help because they are of one family. Also, it is natural for a man to feel more sympathy and pain with his hard-pressed and needy relatives than with strangers. He is humiliated by their degradation and elevated by their honor. Therefore, any well-to-do person who cuts off his kin from assistance and lives in luxury while his relatives are in a state of misery is devoid of natural feeling or lacks belief and is far away from goodness or piety. On the other hand, for one who maintains close links with his kin, his sustenance is assured and his relationship is of beneficence to his kin.

Orphans (wal-yatāmā): In the case of orphans whose guardians have died, their support and upbringing depends on wealthy and well-to-do Muslims so that they will not become a problem to themselves or other people.

The Needy (wal-masākīn): Because they are unable to earn enough to maintain themselves and have become contented with the little they have and abstain from begging, it is necessary for the well-to-do to help them.

Wayfarers (*wab nisabil*): In the case of the wayfarer cut off from family and relatives, as if traveling were his household, consideration requires kindness for him as well. Thus, to sympathize with him and help him in his travels is, within the meaning of Islamic law, an encouragement which invites one to journey throughout the earth.

Beggars (*was-sa'ilīn*): In the case of beggars forced to ask people for their needs, they should be helped. A person may also ask for help in order to redress another's need. However, the *shari'ah* does not approve of begging, except under dire circumstances. Even then, one should not trespass limits.

Slaves (*wa fi ar-riqāb*). The liberation of slaves includes buying and setting them free, helping contracted slaves (*al-mukatabun*) pay off their debts, and helping captives buy their way out of captivity. By encouraging people to spend out of their wealth on slaves, the *shari'ah* wants to emancipate the latter. Still, as important as the emancipation of slaves is, in terms of priorities it is placed at the end, after the orphans, the needy, the wayfarer, and the beggar, the reason being that the former fall under the need for preserving life (which has a higher value), while the latter falls under the right to freedom (a lesser value than life).

The legitimacy of giving *sadaqah* other than that of *zakah* is not restricted by a time limit or definite *nisab*. The amount designated for expenditure need not be a certain percentage (for example, a tithe, a one-quarter tithe, or a one-tenth tithe). It is an open-ended matter that is left to the beneficence, generosity, and condition of the one who gives. The protection of a revered (*muhtaram*) man from destruction and harm is an obligation upon whoever can help him, but more than that, it is left unquantified.

People overlook most of the public rights which the Qur'an supports, for these rights seek to establish an honorable and just social life. People spend only a small amount on the needy and even less for beggars because they are considered the least deserving nowadays. This is due to the fact that beggars have made begging a profession (*hirfah*), even though most of them are well-to-do.

Ibn Hazm says: "It is enjoined upon the rich of every country to support their poor, and the ruler has the authority to force them to do so. This is called for when the prescribed *zakah* or the holdings of other Muslims are not enough to meet the needs of the poor. In that case, their food and their clothing to protect them from the elements and the eyes of the passer-by would be provided by the rich." The proof for this is in the saying of Allah, the Exalted One: "Give the kinsman his due, and the needy, and the wayfarer" [*al-Isra'*: 26]. Allah also says: "[Show] kindness to parents, to near kin and orphans, to the needy, to relatives, to neighbors who are not related to you, to fellow-travelers and wayfarers, and [to the slaves] whom your right hand possesses" [*an-Nisa'*: 36]. Generosity urges support for the above-mentioned people and forbids harming them. Referring to the guilty in the life to come, the Qur'an says that they would ask each other: "What brought you to this hellfire?" They will answer: "We were not of those who prayed, nor did we feed the needy" [*al-Muddaththir*: 42-44]. Thus, Allah links feeding the needy with performing prayers. According to the following *hadith*, related by authentic sources, the Messenger of Allah, upon whom be peace, said: "He who does not have mercy upon people, Allah's mercy will be kept from him." Anyone upon whom Allah bestowed His grace and who sees his Muslim brother hungry, in need of clothes, and miserable, and still does not help him, he will, indeed, deprive himself of Allah's mercy.

'Uthman an-Nahdi reported that 'Abdurrahman ibn Abi Bakr as-Siddiq informed him that the companions of as-Saffah were poor and that the Messenger of Allah, upon whom be peace, said: "He who has enough food for two, let him invite a third, and he who has food for four, let him invite a fifth or a sixth."

It is related from Ibn 'Umar that the Messenger of Allah, upon whom be peace, said: "A Muslim is a brother of another, and he should neither do injustice to him nor betray him." Thus, anyone who lets a needy Muslim go without food or clothes while, in fact, he is able to feed and clothe him would have betrayed him. It is related from Abu Sa'id al-Khudri that the Messenger of Allah, upon whom be peace, said: "He whose holdings exceed his needs, let him support the one whose holdings do not, and he whose food exceeds his needs, let him share it with him who does not have food." Abu Sa'id al-Khudri says: "Then he mentioned so many kinds of property that we thought no one of us had the right to have anything surplus with us." This is the consensus of the companions, as it was reported by Abu Sa'id al-Khudri. Concerning this tradition, it is reported on the authority of Abu Musa al-Ash'ari that the Prophet, upon whom be peace, said: "Feed the hungry, visit the sick, and ransom the prisoner."

There are many 'ayahs in the Qur'an and numerous sound *ahadith* on this subject. 'Umar says: "If I were to live again the past which I have already lived, I would take the surplus from the rich and distribute it among the poor immigrants (*muhajirūn*)." This is considered to be the most authentic report.

'Ali said: "Allah, the Exalted One, has placed a due upon the properties of the rich to meet the needs of the poor. Thus, if the poor go hungry or naked or struggle because of the neglect of the rich, then Allah will hold them [the rich] accountable on the Day of Judgment and will punish them."

Ibn 'Umar is reported to have said: "There is a due on your property other than *zakah*." It is related from 'Aishah (the mother of the believers), al-Hasan ibn 'Ali, Ibn 'Umar that all of them replied to those who had asked them: "If you are asked for help in cases of blood money, heavy debt, or desperate poverty, then it is a must for you to give them from your holdings."

It was accurately reported by Abu 'Ubaidah ibn al-Jarrah and 300 companions that (once) when their provisions had run very low, Abu 'Ubaidah ordered them to collect what was left and place it into two bags and then allot it to each one equally. Then he said: "It is not permissible for a hard-pressed Muslim to eat the meat of a dead animal or a pig when he can find surplus food from either a Muslim or a *dhimmi*. It is an obligation of the one who has food to feed the hungry." This has the consensus among the companions, and there are no contrary views concerning it. It was accurately reported from ash-Shu'bi, Mujahid, Tawus, and others that: "There is a due on property other than *zakah*." If such is the case, then a hard-pressed person is not forced to eat the meat of dead animals or pigs. He has the right to fight for it and, if he is killed, then retaliation by killing (*qawad*) will be imposed upon the killer. If the property holder who prevents him from receiving his due is killed, then may he have the curse of Allah upon him because he withheld a right (*haqq*), and he will be regarded as being among the unjust.

Allah, the Exalted One, says: "And if one party of them does wrong to the other, fight those who do wrong until they return to the ordinance of Allah." Thus, one who withholds a right is an oppressor of his brother. The latter is the possessor of that right. On this basis, Abu Bakr as-Siddiq waged war against those who refused to pay their *zakah*.

From the preceding, one can see the degree of compassion and commiseration that Islam has for the deprived. Islam, in fact, excels over all other faiths and systems. They are like weak, sputtering candles when placed next to the bright and steady light of the sun of Islam.

ZAKAT UT-TATAWWU'
OR VOLUNTARY SADAQAH

Islam calls upon the individual to spend freely in ways that please the heart of the donor, and evoke generosity, goodness, reverence, and obedience to Allah:

From the Qur'an: Allah, the Exalted One, says: "The parable of those who spend their wealth in the way of Allah is that of a grain of corn: it grows seven ears, and each ear has a hundred grains. Allah gives manifold increase to whom He pleases; Allah cares for all and knows all things" [*al-Baqarah*: 261].

"By no means shall you attain righteousness unless you give freely of that which you love, and whatever you give, Allah knows it well" [*āl-'Imran*: 92].

"And spend from what We have made you heir. For those of you who believe and spend, for them is a great reward" [*al-Hadid*: 7].

From the *Hadith*: The Messenger of Allah, upon whom be peace, said: "*Sadaqah* appeases the anger of the Lord and wards off the agony of death."

It is similarly related that the Messenger of Allah, upon whom be peace, said: "The *sadaqah* of the Muslim increases during his lifetime. It also softens the agony of death, and through it, Allah takes away arrogance and vanity."

The Messenger of Allah, upon whom be peace, said: "There is not a day in which the obedient servants rise in the morning or two angels descend, and one of them says: 'O Allah! Compensate the one who spends freely.' The other angel says: 'O Allah! Let an annihilation come upon the one who is niggardly.' " This is related by Muslim.

The Messenger of Allah, upon whom be peace, said: "Acts of kindness protect one from ruin wrought by evil. *Sadaqah* given secretly appeases the anger of the Lord, and a gift to strengthen the ties of relationship increases one's life span. All good deeds are *sadaqah*, and those who do acts of kindness in this world are also the same people in the other world. Those who do misdeeds in this world are the same people in the other world. The first of those who shall enter Paradise are the people who do acts of kindness." This is related by at-Tabarani in *al-'Awsāt*. Mandhiri does not mention it.

Types of *Sadaqah*

Sadaqah is not restricted to any special deed of righteousness. The general rule is that all good deeds are *sadaqah*. Some of them are as follows:

The Messenger of Allah, upon whom be peace, said: "Every Muslim has to give *sadaqah*." The people asked: "O Prophet of Allah, what about the one who has nothing?" He said: "He should work with his hands to give *sadaqah*." They asked: "If he cannot find [work]?" He replied: "He should help the needy who asks for help." They asked: "If he cannot do that?" He replied: "He should then do good deeds and shun evil, for this will be taken as *sadaqah*." This is related by al-Bukhari and others.

The Messenger of Allah, upon whom be peace, said: "*Sadaqah* is prescribed for every person every day the sun rises. To administer justice between two people is *sadaqah*. To assist a man upon his mount so that he may ride it is *sadaqah*. To place his luggage on the animal is *sadaqah*. To remove harm from the road is *sadaqah*. A good word is *sadaqah*. Each step taken toward prayer is *sadaqah*." This is related by Ahmad and others.

Abu Dhar al-Ghafari said: "The Messenger of Allah, upon whom be peace, said: '*Sadaqah* is for every person every day the sun rises.' I said: 'O Messenger of Allah, upon whom be peace, from what do we give *sadaqah* if we do not possess property?' He said: 'The doors of *sadaqah* are *takbir* [i.e., to say: *Allahu-akbar*, Allah is Great]; *Subhan-Allah* [Allah is free from imperfection]; *Alhamdu-*

lillah [all praise is for Allah]; *La -ilaha-illallah* [there is no god other than Allah]; *Astaghfirul-lah* [I seek forgiveness from Allah]; enjoining good; forbidding evil; removing thorns, bones, and stones from the paths of people; guiding the blind; listening to the deaf and dumb until you understand them; guiding a person to his object of need if you know where it is; hurrying with the strength of your legs to one in sorrow who is appealing for help; and supporting the weak with the strength of your arms. These are all the doors of *sadaqah*. [The *sadaqah*] from you is prescribed for you, and there is a reward for you [even] in sex with your wife.' " This is related by Ahmad, and the wording is his. According to Muslim, they said: "O Messenger of Allah, upon whom be peace, is there a reward if one satisfies his passion?" He said: "Do you know that if he satisfies it unlawfully he has taken a sin upon himself? Likewise, if he satisfies it lawfully, he is rewarded."

It is related following Abu Dhar that the Messenger of Allah, upon whom be peace, said: "*Sadaqah* is prescribed for each descendant of Adam every day the sun rises." It was asked: "O Messenger of Allah, upon whom be peace, from what do we give *sadaqah* every day?" He said: "The doors of goodness are many — the *tasbih* [to say '*Subhaan-Allah*'], the *tamhid* [to say '*Al-hamdu lillah*'], the *tahlil* [to say '*La-ilaha-illallah*], enjoining good, forbidding evil, removing harm from the road, listening to the deaf, leading the blind, guiding one to the object of his need, hurrying with the strength of one's legs to one in sorrow who is asking for help, and supporting the feeble with the strength of one's arms — all of these are *sadaqah* prescribed for you." This is related by Ibn Hibban in his *Sahih*. Al-Bukhari related it in a shortened form and added in his report: "Your smile for your brother is *sadaqah*. Your removal of stones, thorns, or bones from the paths of people is *sadaqah*. Your guidance of a person who is lost is *sadaqah*."

The Messenger of Allah also said: "He from among you who is able to protect himself from the Fire should give *sadaqah*, even if but with half a date. If he does not find it, then with a good word."

The Messenger of Allah, upon whom be peace, said: "Allah, the Majestic and Mighty, shall say on the Day of Judgment: 'O son of man! I was ill and you did not visit me.' He will reply: 'O my Lord! How could I visit You and You are the Lord of the Worlds?' Allah shall say: 'Did you not know that My slave, so-and-so, was ill and you did not visit him? If you had visited him, you would have found Me with him. O son of man! I asked you for food and you did not give it to me.' He will reply: 'O my Lord! How could I give You food

— You are the Lord of the Worlds?' Allah shall say: 'Did you not know that My slave, so-and-so, asked you for food and you did not give it to him? Did you not know that if you had given the food, you would have found that with Me? O son of man! I asked you to quench My thirst and you did not.' He will say: 'O my Lord! How could I quench Your thirst — You are the Lord of the Worlds?' Allah shall say: 'My slave, so-and-so, asked you to quench his thirst and you did not. If you had given him to drink, you would have found that with Me.' " This is related by Muslim.

The Messenger of Allah, upon whom be peace, said: "A Muslim does not plant or sow anything from which a person, an animal, or anything eats but it is considered as *sadaqah* from him." This is related by al-Bukhari.

The Messenger of Allah, upon whom be peace, said: "Every good deed is *sadaqah*. To meet your brother with a smiling face and to pour out from your bucket into his container are *sadaqah*."

Those Who Have Precedence for Receiving *Sadaqah*

One's children, family, and relatives have precedence over others. It is not permissible to give *sadaqah* to a stranger when you and your dependents are in need of it.

It is related from Jabir that the Messenger of Allah, upon whom be peace, said: "When one of you is poor, he starts with himself. If anything is left, he spends it on his dependents. If anything is (still left) then on his relatives, and then, if more is left, he spends it here and there."

The Messenger of Allah, upon whom be peace, said: "Give *sadaqah*." A man said: "I have a *dinar*." He replied: "Give it to yourself as *sadaqah*." He said: "I have another *dinar*." He replied: "Give it to your wife as *sadaqah*." He said: "I have another *dinar*." He replied: "Give it to your child as *sadaqah*." He said: "I have another *dinar*." He replied: "Give it to your servant as *sadaqah*." He said: "I have another *dinar*." He replied: "You would be able to assess better [to whom to give it]." This is related by Abu Dawud, an-Nasa'i, and Hakim. Hakim grades it as authentic.

The Messenger of Allah, upon whom be peace, said: "A man has sinned enough if he neglects to feed those in need." This is related by Muslim and Abu Dawud.

Also: "The most excellent *sadaqah* is that given to a relative who does not like you." This is related by at-Tabarani and Hakim. The latter grades it authentic.

The Invalidation of *Sadaqah*

It is unlawful for the one giving *sadaqah* to remind the recipient of his generosity, to reproach him, or to make a show with his *sadaqah*. Allah warns: "O you who believe! Do not invalidate your *sadaqah* by reminders of your generosity or by injury, like those who spend their property to be seen by men" [*al-Baqarah*: 264].

The Messenger of Allah, upon whom be peace, said: "There are three [types of people]. Allah shall not speak to them, notice them, or sanctify them; and for them is a grievous penalty." Abu Dhar inquired: "O Messenger of Allah, who are the ones gone wrong and astray?" He replied: "Those who through conceit lengthen their garments to make them hang on the ground, who give nothing without reproach, and who sell their merchandise swearing untruthfully [to its quality]."

Giving What is Unlawful as *Sadaqah*

Allah does not accept *sadaqah* if it is from what is unlawful: The Messenger of Allah, upon whom be peace, said: "O people! Allah is good and accepts only good, and He has instructed the believers through the Messengers. Allah, the Mighty and the Majestic, says: 'O Messengers! Consume what is good and work righteously. I am well-acquainted with what you do' [*al-Mu'minum*: 51]." He also calls upon [you]: 'O you who believe! Consume of the good that We have provided for you' [*al-Baqarah*: 172]. Then [the Messenger] mentioned a man who had traveled for a long time. Unkempt and covered in dust, he raised his hands to the heavens (and cried): 'O my Lord! O my Lord!' His food was unlawful, his drink was unlawful, his clothing was unlawful, and what he had provided to sustain himself with was also unlawful. How could his invocation be accepted?" This is related by Muslim.

Also: "If one gives a date bought from honestly earned money (and Allah accepts only good), Allah accepts it in His right hand and enlarges [its rewards] for its owner (as one rears his foal) until it becomes as big as a mountain." This is related by al-Bukhari.

The *Sadaqah* of the Wife From the Property of Her Husband

It is permissible for the wife to give *sadaqah* from her husband's holdings if she knows that he would not mind. However, it is unlawful if she is not sure of this: It is related from 'Aishah that the Messenger of Allah, upon whom be peace, said: "When a wife gives something as *sadaqah* from the food of her home without causing any waste, she will get the reward for what she has given. Her husband will be rewarded for what he has earned, and the keeper (if any) will be similarly rewarded. The one does not reduce the reward of the other in any way." This is related by al-Bukhari.

Abu Umamah reports that he had heard the Messenger of Allah, upon whom be peace, saying in a sermon during the year of the Farewell Pilgrimage: "The wife should not spend anything from the household of her husband without his permission." He asked: "O Messenger of Allah, upon whom be peace! Not food either?" He said: "That is the most excellent of our holdings." This is related by at-Tirmidhi who graded it *hassan*.

Of small things which she is in the habit of giving, no permission from her husband is called for: It is related from Asma, daughter of Abu Bakr, that she said to the Messenger of Allah, upon whom be peace: "Zubair is a well-off man. A man in need approached me and I gave him *sadaqah* from ny husband's household without his permission." The Messenger of Allah, upon whom be peace, said: "Give what you are in the habit of giving of what is small, and do not store property away, for Allah shall withhold his blessings from you." This is related by Ahmad, al-Bukhari, and Muslim.

Permissibility of Giving *Sadaqah* of All One's Property

For one who is fit and capable of earning his living, giving *sadaqah* of all his property is permissible.

'Umar reports: "The Messenger of Allah, upon whom be peace, instructed us to give *sadaqah*, and it applied to my property. I said: 'Today I shall better Abu Bakr. I have never bettered him.' Then I brought half my property. The Messenger of Allah, upon whom be peace, said: 'What did you leave for your family?' I said: 'An amount like this.' Abu Bakr came with all his property, and the

Messenger of Allah, upon whom be peace, asked: 'What did you leave for your family?' He said: 'I have left Allah and His Messenger, upon whom be peace, for them.' Then I said: 'I shall never better you in anything.'" This is related by Abu Dawud and at-Tirmidhi. The latter grades it authentic.

Giving all of one's property: The jurists say that giving all of one's property in *sadaqah* is permissible provided the donor is fit, earning, and steadfast, not in debt, nor has dependents for whom adequate support from him is obligatory. If he does not fulfil these conditions, then his action is *makruh*.

Jabir narrated: "While we were with the Messenger of Allah, upon whom be peace, a man came with what was like an egg of gold. He said: 'O Messenger of Allah! I obtained this from buried treasure, so take it. It is *sadaqah*, and I do not possess anything other than it.' The Messenger of Allah, upon whom be peace, turned away from him and he [the man] then approached him from the direction of his left side. The Messenger of Allah, upon whom be peace, then turned away from him again and he approached him from behind. Then the Messenger of Allah, upon whom be peace, took it and threw it at him. If it had hit him, it would have injured him. Then he said: 'One of you comes with all his property to make *sadaqah*, then after [giving all he had] he sits [by the road] begging from the people. *Sadaqah* is given by the one who is rich.'" This is related by Abu Dawud and Hakim. The latter said: "It is authentic according to the stipulation of Muslim. In its transcription is Muhammad ibn Ishaq."

Giving *Sadaqah* to the *Dhimmi* and the Soldier

One can give *sadaqah* to the *dhimmi* and the soldier, and one is rewarded for that. Allah praised a group of people (for this) when He said: "And they feed, for His love, the indigent, orphan, and captive" [*ad-Dahr*: 6]. The captive is a soldier. Allah says: "Allah has not forbidden you with regard to those who have not made war against you on account of [your] faith and have not driven you out of your homes to deal kindly and justly with them; Allah loves those who are just" [*al-Mumtahanah*: 8].

Asma, the daughter of Abu Bakr, reports: "My mother came to me and she is a polytheist. I said: 'O Messenger of Allah, upon whom be peace! If my mother came to me and she is willing, do I establish a link with her?' He said: 'Yes, establish a link with your mother.' "

Sadaqah on Animals

The Messenger of Allah, upon whom be peace, is reported to have said: "While a man was walking along a road, he became very thirsty and found a well. He lowered himself into the well, drank, and came out. Then [he saw] a dog protruding its tongue out with thirst. The man said: 'This dog has become exhausted from thirst in the same way as I.' He lowered himself into the well again and filled his shoe with water. Then he took the dog by the mouth until he had raised himself. He gave the dog some water to drink. He thanked Allah, and [his sins were] forgiven." They asked: "O Messenger of Allah, upon whom be peace! Is there a reward for us in our animals?" He said: "There is a reward in every living thing." This is related by al-Bukhari and Muslim.

The two also related that the Messenger of Allah, upon whom be peace, said: "While a dog was walking around a well, his thirst was near to killing him. One of the prostitutes of the Banu Isra'il saw him. She took off her shoe and drew water for him with it in order to quench his thirst. [For that] she was forgiven [by Allah]."

The perpetual *sadaqah* (*sadaqat ul-jariyah*): Ahmad and Muslim relate that the Messenger of Allah, upon whom be peace, said: "When a person dies [the benefit] of his deeds ends, except three: a continuous *sadaqah*, knowledge from which benefit is derived, or a pious child invoking Allah for him."

Thanking for a Good Deed

'Abdullah ibn 'Umar reports that the Messenger of Allah, upon whom be peace, said: "Whoever seeks the protection of Allah, give him protection. Whoever asks you in the name of Allah, grant him refuge. Whoever does a good deed to you, reward him and if you do not find anything, invoke Allah on his behalf until you know that he has been rewarded." This is related by Abu Dawud and an-Nasa'i with an authentic chain.

Ashab ibn Qais reported that the Messenger of Allah, upon whom be peace, is reported to have said: "Whoever does not thank people, does not thank Allah." This is related by Ahmad with a trustworthy chain.

Usamah ibn Zaid adds that the Messenger of Allah, upon whom be peace, said: "To whom a good deed is done and who says to its doer: 'May Allah reward you with goodness,' also reaps the reward." This is related by at-Tirmidhi.

Allah is the Most Knowing, and all praise is due to the Lord of the Worlds.

Part II as-Siyām and i'tikāf

O you who believe! Fasting is ordained for you as it was ordained for those before you, so that you [learn] self-restraint.

Fast for a fixed number of days. But if any of you is ill, or on a journey, the prescribed number [should be made up] from days later; and [in such cases] it is incumbent upon those who can afford it to feed a needy person. And whoever gives more, of his own free will, does good to himself. And it is better for you to fast, if you only knew (al-Baqarah: 183-184).

FASTING (*AS-SIYĀM*)

As-Siyām generally means "to abstain from something." For example, a verse in the Qur'ān says: "I have vowed to the Merciful to abstain — that is, from speaking.

What is meant here is abstaining from food, drink, and sexual intercourse from dawn until sunset with the explicit intention of doing so (for the sake of Allah).

The Virtues of Fasting: Abu Hurairah reported the Messenger of Allah, upon whom be peace, saying: "Allah said: 'Every action of the son of Adam is for him except fasting, for that is solely for Me. I give the reward for it.' The fast is a shield. If one is fasting, he should not use foul language, raise his voice, or behave foolishly. If someone reviles him or fights with him he should say, 'I am fasting,' twice. By the One in whose hand is the soul of Muhammad, the [bad] breath of the one who is fasting is better in the sight of Allah on the Day of Resurrection than the smell of musk. The one who is fasting is happy at two times: when he breaks his fast he is happy with it, and when he meets his Lord he will be happy that he has fasted." This is related by Ahmad, Muslim, and an-Nasa'i. A similar version was recorded by al-Bukhari and Abu Dawud, but with the following addition: "He leaves his food, drink, and desires for My sake. His fasting is for Me, . . . I will give the reward for it, and for every good deed, he will receive ten similar to it."

'Abdullah ibn 'Amr reported that the Messenger of Allah, upon whom be peace, said: "The fast and the Qur'an are two intercessors for the servant of Allah on the Day of Resurrection. The fast will say: 'O Lord, I prevented him from his food and desires during the day. Let me intercede for him.' The Qur'an will say: 'I prevented him from sleeping at night. Let me intercede for him.' And their intercession will be accepted." Ahmad related this *hadith* with a *sahih* chain.

Abu Umamah reported: "I came to the Messenger of Allah and said: 'Order me to do a deed that will allow me to enter Paradise.' He said: 'Stick to fasting, as there is no equivalent to it.' Then I came to him again and he said: 'Stick to fasting.'" This *hadith* is related by Ahmad, an-Nasa'i, and al-Hakim who classified it as *sahih*.

Abu Sa'id al-Khudri reported that the Messenger of Allah said: "No servant fasts on a day in the path of Allah except that Allah removes the hellfire seventy years further away from his face." This is related by "the group," except for Abu Dawud.

Sahl ibn Sa'd reported that the Prophet said: "There is a gate to Paradise that is called ar-Rayyan. On the Day of Resurrection it will say: 'Where are those who fasted?' When the last [one] has passed through the gate, it will be locked." This is related by al-Bukhari and Muslim.

Types of Fasting: There are two types of fasting: obligatory and voluntary. Obligatory can be further subdivided into the fast of Ramadān, the fast of expiation and the fast of fulfilling a vow. Here we shall discuss the Ramadan and voluntary fasts.

The Fast of Ramadan

The fast of Ramadan, according to the Qur'an, *sunnah* and consensus, is obligatory.

The evidence from the Qur'an consists of the following two verses: "O you who believe, fasting is prescribed for you as it was prescribed for the people before you in order for you to gain God-consciousness, and, "...The month of Ramadan, during which the Qur'an was revealed, a guidance for mankind, and clear proofs of the guidance and the criterion; and whoever of you is resident, let him fast the month" [al-Baqarah: 185].

From the *sunnah* we have the following statements of the Prophet: "Islam is built upon [the following] five pillars: testifying that there is no God except Allah and that Muhammad is His Messenger, the establishment of the prayer, the giving of *zakah*, the fast of

Ramadan and the pilgrimage to Makkah." Talhah ibn 'Ubaidullah reported that a man came to the Prophet and said: "O Messenger of Allah, tell me what Allah requires of me as regards fasting." He answered, "The month of Ramadan." The man asked: "Is there any other [fast]?" The Prophet answered: "No, unless you do so voluntarily."

The whole Muslim nation agrees that the fast of Ramadan is obligatory. It is one of the pillars of Islam, and if one disputes this, he cannot be called a Muslim.[1]

The Virtues of Ramadan and the Deeds Done During It

Abu Hurairah reported that the Prophet, upon whom be peace, said: "The blessed month has come to you. Allah has made fasting during it obligatory upon you. During it, the gates to Paradise are opened and the gates to hellfire are locked, and the devils are chained. There is a night [during this month] which is better than a thousand months. Whoever is deprived of its good is really deprived [of something great]." This is related by Ahmad, an-Nasa'i, and al-Baihaqi.

'Arfajah testifies to this: "We were with 'Utbah ibn Farqad while he was discussing Ramadan. A companion of the Prophet entered upon the scene. When 'Utbah saw him, he became shy and stopped talking. The man [the companion] spoke about Ramadan, saying: 'I heard the Messenger of Allah say during Ramadan: "The gates of Hell are closed, the gates of Paradise are opened, and the devils are in chains. An angel calls out: 'O you who intend to do good deeds, have glad tidings. O you who intend to do evil, refrain, until Ramadan is completed.' "

Muslim relates that Abu Hurairah reported the Prophet saying: "The time between the five prayers, two consecutive Friday prayers, and two consecutive Ramadans are expiations for all that has happened during that period, provided that one has avoided the grave sins."

Abu Sa'id al-Khudri reported that the Prophet, upon whom be peace, said: "Whoever fasts the month of Ramadan, obeying all of its limitations and guarding himself against what is forbidden, has in fact atoned for any sins he committed before it." Ahmad and al-Baihaqi related this *hadith* with a good chain.

---

[1] It was made obligatory during the year 2 A.H.

Abu Hurairah reported that the Prophet, upon whom be peace, said: "Whoever fasts the month of Ramadan with faith and seeks Allah's pleasure and reward will have his previous sins forgiven." This *hadith* is related by Ahmad and the compilers of the *sunan*.

The Consequence of Breaking the Fast of Ramadan

Ibn 'Abbas reported that the Prophet said: "The bare essence of Islam and the basics of the religion are three [acts], upon which Islam has been established. Whoever leaves one of them becomes an unbeliever and his blood may legally be spilled. [The acts are:] Testifying that there is no God except Allah, the obligatory prayers, and the fast of Ramadan." This *hadith* is related by Abu Ya'la and ad-Dailimi. Adh-Dhahabi called it *sahih*.[2]

Abu Hurairah reported that the Messenger of Allah, upon whom be peace, said: "Whoever breaks his fast during Ramadan without having one of the excuses that Allah would excuse him for, then even a perpetual fast, if he were to fast it, would not make up for that day." This is related by Abu Dawud, Ibn Majah, and at-Tirmidhi.

Al-Bukhari records from Abu Hurairah in *marfu'* form: "Whoever breaks the fast of Ramadan without having a legitimate excuse or being ill, he cannot make up for that day, even if he were to undertake a perpetual fast." Ibn Mas'ud has also reported this.[3]

---

[2]Although al-Mundhiri and al-Haithami say that this *hadith's* chain is *hassan*, it is definitely weak. Al-Albani has discussed this *hadith* in detail in *Silsilat al-Ahadith adh-Dha'eefah*, number 84. Most likely it is a statement of Ibn 'Abbas. In fact in *Kitab al-Kaba'ir*, adh-Dhahabi has recorded it only as a statement of Ibn 'Abbas, and not as a *hadith* of the Prophet (cf. *Kitab al-Kaba'ir*, Dar an-Nadwah wa al-Jadeem, Beirut, p. 38). J.Z.

[3]Although this *hadith* was recorded by at-Tirmidhi, Abu Dawud, an-Nasa'i, Ibn Majah, Ibn Khuzaimah and others, it is weak, as al-Albani mentioned in his *takhreej* of *Mishkat al-Masabih* and as 'Abdul Qader al-Arnaut mentions in his *takhreej* of *Ami' al-Usul fi Ahadith ar-Rasool*. At-Tirmidhi said: "This *hadith* of Abu Hurairah is known to us only through this chain. I heard Muhammad [that is al-Bukhari] say, Abu al-Matus' name is Yazid ibn al-Matus, and I don't know of any other *hadith* from him." Although al-Bukhari recorded this in his *Sahih*, he recorded it in *mu'allaq* form with a *sighat at-tamreedh*, which shows that he considered it weak. For a complete discussion on this *hadith*, see Ibn Hajr, *Fath al-Bari* (Ministry of Islamic Research, Dawah, Saudi Arabia), vol. 4 pp. 160 f. J.Z.

Adh-Dhahabi says: "According to the established believers, anyone who leaves the fast of Ramadan without being sick is worse than a fornicator or an alcoholic. In fact, they doubt his Islam and they suspect that he might be a *zandiqah*[4] and one of those who destroy [Islam].

The Arrival of Ramadan

This event is confirmed by sighting the new moon, even if it is seen by only one just person, or by the passage of thirty days in the immediately preceding month of Sha'ban.

Ibn 'Umar said: "The people were looking for the new moon and when I reported to the Messenger of Allah that I had seen it, he fasted and ordered the people to fast." This is related by Abu Dawud, al-Hakim, and Ibn Hibban, who declared it to be *sahih*.

Abu Hurairah reported that the Prophet instructed: "Fast after you have seen it [the new crescent] and end the fast [at the end of the month] when you see it. If it is hidden from you, then wait until the thirty days of Sha'ban have passed." This is related by al-Bukhari and Muslim.

Commenting on these reports, at-Tirmidhi states: "Most knowledgeable people act in accordance with these reports. They say that it is correct to accept the evidence of one person to determine the beginning of the fast. This is the opinion of Ibn al-Mubarak, ash-Shaf'i, and Ahmad. An-Nawawi says that it is the soundest opinion. Concerning the new moon of Shawwal [which signifies the end of the fast], it is confirmed by completing thirty days of Ramadan, and most jurists state that the new moon must have been reported by at least two just witnesses. However, Abu Thaur does not distinguish between the new moon of Shawwal and the new moon of Ramadan. In both cases, he accepts the evidence of only one just witness."

Ibn-Rushd comments that: "The opionion of Abu Bakr ibn al-Mundhir, which is also that of Abu Thaur and, I suspect, that of the Dhahiri school of thought, is supported by the following argument given by Abu Bakr al-Mundhiri: there is complete agreement that breaking the fast is obligatory, that abstaining from eating is based on one person's report, and that the situation must be like that for the beginning of the month and for the ending of the month, as both

---

[4]Those who claimed to be Muslim so that they could destroy it from within. J.Z.

of them are simply the signs that differentiate the time of fasting from the time of not fasting."

Ash-Shaukani observes: "If there is nothing authentic recorded that states that one may only accept two witnesses for the end of the month, then it is apparent, by analogy, that one witness is sufficient, as it is sufficient for the beginning of the month. Furthermore, worship based on the acceptance of one report points to the fact that such singular reports are accepted in every matter unless there is some evidence that specifies the peculiarity of specific cases, such as the number of witnesses concerning matters of wealth, and so on. Apparently this is the opinion of Abu Thaur."

Different Locations

According to the majority of scholars, it does not matter if the new moon has been sighted in a different location. In other words, after the new moon is seen anywhere in the world, it becomes obligatory for all Muslims to begin fasting, as the Prophet said: "Fast due to its sighting and break the fast due to its sighting." This *hadith* is a general address directed to the whole Muslim world – that is, "if any one of you sees the moon in any place, then that will be a sighting for all of the people."

According to 'Ikrimah, al-Qasim ibn Muhammad, Salim, Ishaq, the correct opinion among the Hanafiyyah, and the chosen opinion among the Shaf'iyyah, every "country" (or territory) is to take into consideration its own sighting and not necessarily to follow the sighting of others. This is based on what Kuraib said: "While I was in ash-Sham, the new moon of Ramadan appeared on Thursday night. I returned to Madinah at the end of the month. There, Ibn 'Abbas asked me: 'When did you people see the new moon?' I said: 'We saw it on Thursday night.' He said: 'Did you see it yourself?' I said: 'Yes, the people saw it, and they and Mu'awiyyyah fasted.' He said: 'But we saw it on Friday night. We will not stop fasting until we complete thirty days or until we see the new moon.' I said: 'Isn't Mu'awiyyah's sighting and fasting sufficient for you?' He said: 'No ... This is the order of the Messenger of Allah.' " This is related by Ahmad, Muslim, and at-Tirmidhi.

About the *hadith*, at-Tirmidhi says: "It is *hassan sahih ghareeb*. Scholars act in accordance with this *hadith*. Every land has its sighting." In *Fath al-'Alam Sharh Bulugh al-Maram*, it is stated: The [opinion] closest [to the truth] is that each land follows its sighting, as well as the areas that are connected to it."

Sighting of the Crescent by one Person

The scholars of *fiqh* agree that if only one person sees the new moon, he is to fast. 'Ata differs and says that he is not to fast until someone else also sights the new moon with him. The correct position is that he is to break the fast, as ash-Shaf'i and Abu Thaur have ruled. The Prophet has based the fast and its breaking on the sighting of the moon. One's own sight is enough for him and there is no need for another person's sighting.

The Essential Elements of the Fast

The fast has two essential elements (literally, "pillars") that must be fulfilled for it to be valid and acceptable. They are:

Abstaining from those acts that break the fast: This point is based on the Qur'anic verse: "Eat and drink until the white thread becomes distinct to you from the black thread of the dawn. Then strictly observe the fast until nightfall."

This is also based on the following *hadith*: "When the verse 'Eat and drink until the white thread becomes distinct to you ...' was revealed, I took a black thread and a white thread and placed them underneath my pillow. During the night I looked at them to see if I could distinguish between them. In the morning I went to the Messenger of Allah and mentioned that to him and he said: 'It is the black of the night and the white of the day.' "

The intention: Allah instructs in the Qur'an: "And they are ordained nothing else than to serve Allah, keeping religion pure for Him." The Prophet, upon whom be peace, said: "Actions are judged according to the intention behind them, and for everyone is what he intended."

The intention must be made before *fajr* and during every night of Ramadan. This point is based on the *hadith* of Hafsah which reported that the Prophet said: "Whoever does not determine to fast before *fajr* will have no fast" (that is, it won't be accepted). This is related by Ahmad, an-Nasa'i, at-Tirmidhi, Abu Dawud, and Ibn Majah. Ibn Khuzaimah and Ibn Hibban have classified it as *sahih*.

The intention is valid during any part of the night. It need not be spoken, as it is in reality an act of the heart which does not involve the tongue. It will be fulfilled by one's intention to fast out of obedience to Allah and for seeking His pleasure.

If one eats one's pre-dawn meal (*sahoor*) with the intention of fasting and to get closer to Allah by such abstinence, then one has performed the intention. If one determines that one will fast on the next day solely for the sake of Allah, then one has performed the intention even if a pre-dawn meal was not consumed.

According to many of the jurists, the intention for a voluntary fast may be made at any time before any food is consumed. This opinion is based on 'Aishah's *hadith*: "The Prophet came to us one day and said: 'Do you have any [food]?' We said, 'No.' He said: 'Therefore, I am fasting." This is related by Muslim and Abu Dawud.

The Hanafiyyah and Shaf'iyyah stipulate that the intention must be made before noon (for voluntary fasts). The apparent opinion of Ibn Mas'ud and Ahmad is that the intention may be made before or after noon.

Who must fast: All scholars agree that fasting is obligatory upon every sane, adult, healthy Muslim male who is not traveling at that time. As for a woman, she must not be menstruating or having post-childbirth bleeding. People who are insane, minors, and those who are traveling, menstruating, or going through post-childbirth bleeding, and the elderly and breast-feeding or pregnant women do not need to observe the fast.

For some, the fast is not obligatory at all, for example, the insane. In the case of young people, their parents or guardians should order them to fast. Some are to break the fast and make up the missed days of fasting at a later date, while others are to break the fast and pay a "ransom" (in which case, they are not obliged to make up the days they missed). We shall discuss each group in more detail.

The fast of the insane: Fasting is not obligatory for the insane because of their inability to understand what they are doing. 'Ali reported that the Prophet, upon whom be peace, said: "The pen is raised for three groups [of people] — that is, they will not be responsible for their actions: the insane until they become sane, those who are sleeping until they awaken, and the young until they reach puberty." This is related by Ahmad, Abu Dawud, and at-Tirmidhi.

The fast of the young [non-adults]: Though the young are not required to fast, it is proper for their guardians to encourage them to fast so they will become accustomed to it at an early age. They may fast as long as they are able to and then may break it. Ar-Rabi'a bint Mu'awiyyah reported: "The Messenger of Allah sent a man, on the morning of the day of 'Ashurah, to the residences of the *Ansar*, saying: 'Whoever has spent the morning fasting is to complete his fast. Whoever has not spent this morning fasting should fast for the remainder of the day.' We fasted after that announcement, as did our young children. We would go to the mosque and make toys stuffed with cotton for them to play with. If one of them started crying due to hunger, we would give them a toy to play with until it was time to eat." This is related by al-Bukhari and Muslim.

Those who are permitted to break the fast, but who must pay a "ransom" for not fasting: Elderly men and women are permitted to break their fasts, as are the chronically ill, and those who have to perform difficult jobs under harsh circumstances and who could not find any other way to support themselves. All of these people are allowed to break their fast, because such a practice would place too much hardship on them during any part of the year. They are obliged to feed one poor person [*miskin*] a day (for every day of fasting that they do not perform). The scholars differ over how much food is to be supplied, for example, a *sa'*, half a *sa'*, or a *madd*.[5] There is nothing in the *sunnah* that mentions exactly how much is to be given.

Ibn 'Abbas said: "An elderly man is permitted to break his fast, but he must feed a poor person daily. If he does this, he does not have to make up the days that he did not fast. This is related by ad-Daraqutni and by al-Hakim, who said it is *sahih*. Al-Bukhari recorded that 'Ata heard Ibn 'Abbas recite the *'ayah*: "And for those who can fast [but do not], there is a "ransom': the feeding of a person in need" [*al-Baqarah*: 185]. Then Ibn 'Abbas continued: "It has not been abrogated. [Its ruling applies] to elderly men and women who are not able to fast. Instead, they must feed one poor person on a daily basis."

The same is true for one who is chronically ill and as such cannot fast, and for one who is forced to work under harsh circumstances and as such cannot endure the additional burden of fasting. Both groups must also feed one poor person daily.

---

[5]*Sa'* and *madd* are two types of measurement. A *sa'* is equal to four *madd*. A *madd* is equal to what a man with an average-size hand can hold in his two hands. J.Z.

Commenting on *al-Baqarah's 'ayah*, Sheikh Muhammad 'Abduh says: "What is meant by those who can fast' [(but do not) in the Qur'anic verse] is the weak elderly people, the chronically ill, and so on, and similarly, those workers who are working under severe conditions, such as coal miners. The same applies to criminals who are sentenced to life imprisonment with hard labor. They have to pay the 'ransom' if they have the means to do so."

Pregnant and breast-feeding women, if they fear for themselves or for the baby, can break the fast and pay the "ransom." They do not have to make up the days missed. Abu Dawud related from 'Ikrimah that Ibn 'Abbas said concerning the *'ayah* "And for those who can fast [but do not],": "This is a concession for the elderly, as they can fast. They are to break the fast and feed one poor person a day. Pregnant or breast-feeding women, if they fear for the child, can do likewise." This is related by al-Bazzar. At the end of the report, there is the addition: "Ibn 'Abbas used to say to his wives who were pregnant: 'You are in the same situation as those who can fast [but do not]. You are to pay the "ransom" and do not have to make up the days later.' " Of its chain, ad-Daraqutni says it is *sahih*.

Nafi' reported that Ibn 'Umar was asked about a pregnant woman who feared for her unborn baby. He replied: "She is to break the fast and to feed one poor person a day one *madd* of barley."

There is also a *hadith* that states: "Allah has relieved the travelers of fasting and half of the prayer, and the pregnant and the breast-feeding women of the fast."[6]According to the Hanafiyyah, Abu Ubaid, and Abu Thaur, such women are only to make up the missed days of fasting, and they are not supposed to feed one poor person a day. According to Ahmad and ash-Shaf'i, if such women fear only for the baby, they must pay the "ransom" and make up the days later. If they fear only for themselves or for themselves and the baby, then they are only to make up the missed days at a later date.

Making up the Missed Days of Fasting

It is allowed for those who are (not chronically) ill and for travelers to break their fasts during Ramadan, but they must make

---

[6]This *hadith* was related by at-Tirmidhi, Abu Dawud, an-Nasa'i, and Ibn Majah. Its chain is *hassan*. J.Z.

up the days they missed. Allah says in the Qur'an: "And [for] him who is sick among you or on a journey, [the same] number of other days."

Mu'adh said: "Verily, Allah made the fast obligatory upon the Prophet by revealing: 'O you who believe, fasting is prescribed for you as it was prescribed for those before you . . .' until the words, 'And for those who can fast [but do not] there is a "ransom" payment. . .' Then, whoever wished to do so would fast and whoever wished to do so would feed a poor person, and that was sufficient for them. Then Allah revealed another verse: 'The month of Ramadan in which the Qur'an was revealed . . .' to the words: 'Whoever is resident among you during this month is to fast.' [By this verse,] the fast was established for those who were resident and healthy. A concession was made for the sick and travelers, and the feeding of the poor by the elderly who could not fast was [left] confirmed." This is related by Ahmad, Abu Dawud, and al-Baihaqi with a *sahih* chain.

A sick person may break his fast which, if continued, would only aggravate the illness or delay its cure.[7] In *al-Mughni* it is stated: "It is related from some of the early scholars that any type of illness allows one to break the fast, even an injury to the finger or a toothache. They based their opinion on the following: (a) the wording of the verse is general and applies to all types of illness, and (b) a traveler is allowed to break his fast even if he does not need to and, therefore, the same must be the case for one who is sick." This was also the opinion of al-Bukhari, 'Ata, and the Dhahiri school of thought.

One who is healthy but fears that he will become ill if he fasts can break the fast, as can the person who is overcome by hunger and/or thirst and fears that he may die because of it, even if he is resident and healthy. He must make up the days of fasting that he missed. The following two Qur'anic *'ayahs* support this point: "And do not kill yourselves, Lo! Allah is ever Merciful to you," and "He has not laid upon you in your religion any hardship."

If a sick person fasts and withstands the hardships of the fast, his fast will be valid but disliked, for he did not accept the concession Allah gave him, thereby causing himself much hardship. Some of the companions would fast during the Prophet's lifetime while

---

[7]This could be determined by experience or by consultation with a trustworthy physician, or if there is enough evidence to suggest that one would become ill. Sabiq's footnote.

others would not (that is, if they were ill), thereby following the verdict of the Prophet. Hamzah al-Aslami said: "O Messenger of Allah, I find within me the strength to fast while traveling. Would there be any blame upon me if I were to do so?" The Prophet, upon whom be peace, answered: "It is a concession from Allah. Whoever takes it has done well. Whoever likes to fast, there is no blame upon him." This is related by Muslim.

Abu Sa'id al-Khudri reported: "We traveled with the Messenger of Allah to Makkah while we were fasting. We stopped at a place and the Messenger of Allah said: 'You are coming close to your enemies. You will be stronger if you break the fast.' That was a concession and some of us fasted and some of us broke our fasts. Then we came to another place and the Prophet said: 'In the morning you will face your enemy. Breaking the fast will give you more strength.' So we broke our fast, taking that as the best course of action. After that, you could see some of us fasting with the Prophet while traveling." This is related by Ahmad, Muslim, and Abu Dawud.

In another report, Abu Sa'id al-Khudri said: "We fought under the leadership of the Messenger of Allah during Ramadan. Some of us fasted and some of us did not. The ones who fasted did not find any fault with those who did not fast, and those who did not fast found no fault with those who fasted. They knew that if one had the strength to fast he could do so and it was good, and that if one was weak, he was allowed to break his fast, and that was good." This is related by Ahmad and Muslim.

The jurists differ over what is preferred (that is, to fast or not to fast while traveling). Abu Hanifah, ash-Shaf'i, and Malik are of the opinion that if one has the ability to fast, it is better for him to do so, and if one does not have the ability to fast, it is better for him to break the fast. Ahmad said that it is best to break the fast. 'Umar ibn 'Abdulaziz says: "The best of the two acts is the easier of the two. If it is easier for one to fast than to make up the day later on, then, in his case, to fast is better."

Ash-Shaukani has concluded that if it is difficult for an individual to fast or to reject the concession, then it is best for him not to fast (while traveling). Similarly, if one fears that one's fasting during travel will look like showing off, then in this case, breaking the fast would be preferred. If one is not faced with such conditions, then fasting would be preferred.

If a traveler makes the intention (to fast) during the night, he can still break his fast during the day. Jabir ibn 'Abdullah reported:

"The Messenger of Allah left for Makkah during the year of the conquest [of Makkah] and he and the people with him fasted until he reached a certain valley. He then called for a cup of water, which he elevated so that the people could see it, and then he drank. Afterwards, he was told that some people had continued to fast, and he said: 'Those are disobedient ones, those are disobedient ones.' " This is related by Muslim, at-Tirmidhi, and an-Nasa'i. At-Tirmidhi called it *sahih*.

If one has already made the intention to fast while resident but then decided to travel during the day, the majority of scholars maintain that he must fast. Ahmad and Ishaq say that he may break the fast. This opinion is based on the report of Muhammad ibn Ka'b who said: "I came to Anas ibn Malik during Ramadan while he was planning on traveling. His mount was prepared for him, and he was wearing his clothes for traveling. He asked for some food and ate. I said to him: 'Is this a *sunnah?*' He said, 'Yes.' Then he mounted his animal and left." This is related by at-Tirmidhi, who called it *hassan.*[8]'Ubaid ibn Jubair said: "During Ramadan, I rode on a ship with Abu Basra al-Ghafari from al-Fustat. He prepared his food and said, "Come [and eat]." I said: "Are we not still among the houses [of the city – that is, they had not left yet]?" Abu Basra asked: "Are you turning away from the *sunnah* of the Messenger of Allah?" This is related by Ahmad and Abu Dawud. Its narrators are trustworthy.

Ash-Shaukani contends: "These two *ahadith* prove that a traveler may break his fast before he begins his journey. Of its credentials, Ibn al-'Arabi says: 'Concerning the *hadith* of Anas, it is *sahih* and proves that one can break the fast when he is prepared to travel.' " This is the correct position.

The type of travel that allows one to break his fast is the same as the traveling which allows one to shorten the prayers. We have discussed all of the opinions on this point under the section *Shortening the Prayers*, and we have also recorded Ibn al-Qayyim's conclusions on this question.

Ahmad, Abu Dawud, al-Baihaqi, and at-Tahawi recorded from Mansur al-Kalbi that Dihya ibn Khalifah traveled a distance of one *farsakh* during Ramadan. When he broke his fast, some of the people accompanying him did likewise. Some of them did not agree with this action. On his return to his city, Dihya said: "I saw some-

---

[8]In the chain of this *hadith* there is 'Ubaid ibn Ja'far, who is a weak narrator. J.Z.

thing today that I did not suspect I would ever see. The people turned away the Messenger of Allah's guidance and that of his companions." He said that about the people who had fasted. Then he said: "O Allah, take [my soul] to you." All of its narrators are trustworthy, except for Mansur al-Kalbi ... although al-'Ijli affirms his credibility.

Those who must make up the missed days: The scholars agree that it is obligatory for menstruating women and women with postchildbirth bleeding to break the fast and to make up the missed days later on. Al-Bukhari and Muslim recorded that 'Aishah said: "When we would have our menses during the lifetime of the Prophet, we were ordered to make up the days of fasting that we had missed but were not ordered to make up the prayers that we had missed.

The Forbidden Days to Fast

There are some *ahadith* that explicitly prohibit fasting on certain days. These are:

(1) The days of *'id*: All scholars agree that such a fast is prohibited. It does not matter if the fast is obligatory or voluntary. 'Umar testifies: "The Messenger of Allah has forbidden fasting on these two days. Concerning the *'id* of breaking the fast, it is for you to break your fast [of Ramadan]. On the *'id* of sacrifice, you should eat from what you sacrifice." This is related by Ahmad, an-Nasa'i, at-Tirmidhi, Abu Dawud, and Ibn Majah.

(2) The days of *tashreeq* (that is, the three days following the *'Id al-Adha*): It is not permissible to fast during the three days following the *'Id al-Adha*. Abu Hurairah reported that the Messenger of Allah, upon whom be peace, sent 'Abdullah ibn Hudhaqah to announce at Mina: "You are not to fast these days. They are days of eating and drinking and remembering Allah." This is related by Ahmad with a good chain.

Ibn 'Abbas reported that the Messenger of Allah, upon whom be peace, sent a person to announce: "Do not fast on these days, as they are days of eating, drinking and rejoicing with one's family." At-Tabarani related it in *al-'Awsat*.

The Shaf'iyyah allow fasting on the days of *tashreeq* if there is some reason for the fasting — that is, if it is due to an oath, for expiation, or for making up a missed day of Ramadan. Those fasts that have no special reason behind them are not allowed, and there is no disagreement on this point. The Shaf'iyyah applied the same reasoning that they used in saying that prayers that are performed for a specific reason are allowed to be performed during the prohibited times of prayer [for example, the prayer of salutation to the mosque, and so on].

(3) It is prohibited to single out Friday as a day of fasting: The day of Friday is a kind of weekly *'id* for Muslims and, therefore, it is prohibited to fast on that day. Most scholars say that this prohibition is one of dislike,[9] not one of complete forbiddance.

If one fasts on the day before or after it, or if it is a day that one customarily fasts on (for example, the 13th, 14th, or 15th of the month), or if it is the day of 'Arafah or 'Ashurah, then it is not disliked to fast on such a Friday.

'Abdullah ibn 'Amr reported that the Messenger of Allah entered the room of Juwairiyah bint al-Harith while she was fasting on a Friday. He asked her: "Did you fast yesterday?" She answered, "No." He said: "Do you plan to fast tomorrow?" She answered, "No." Therefore he said: "Then break your fast." This is related by Ahmad and an-Nasa'i with a good chain.

'Amr al-'Ashari reported that he heard the Messenger of Allah say: "Verily, Friday is an *'id* for you, so do not fast on it unless you fast the day before or after it." This is related by al-Bazzar with a good chain.

'Ali counseled: "He who wants to [fast] voluntarily should fast on Thursday instead of Friday, for Friday is a day of eating, drinking, and remembrance." This is related by Ibn Abu Shaibah with a good chain.

In the two *Sahih* (those of al-Bukhari and Muslim), Jabir reported that the Prophet said: "Do not fast on Friday unless you fast on it together with the day before or the day after." Muslim's version states: "Do not exclusively choose the night of Friday [Thursday night in English] as a special night for performing the night prayers. Also, do not exclusively choose Friday as a day of fasting unless it occurs on a day that you regularly fast."

---

[9]According to Abu Hanifah and Malik, it is not disliked, but the evidence presented disagrees with their opinion on this matter.

It is prohibited to single out Saturday as a day of fasting: Busr as-Salmi related from his sister as-Sama' that the Messenger of Allah, upon whom be peace, said: "Do not fast on Saturdays unless it is an obligatory fast. [You should not fast] even if you do not find anything [to eat] save some grape peelings or a branch of a tree to chew on."

This is related by Ahmad, an-Nasa'i, at-Tirmidhi, Abu Dawud, Ibn Majah, and al-Hakim. Al-Hakim said that it is *sahih* according to the conditions of Muslim, while at-Tirmidhi called it *hassan*. At-Tirmidhi said that what is disliked here is for a person to exclusively choose Saturday as a day of fasting, as it is the day that the Jews honor.

In contradiction with the preceding report, Umm Salamah claims: "The Prophet used to fast more often on Saturdays and Sundays than on the other days. He would say: 'They are the *'ids* of the polytheists, and I love to differ from them.' " This is related by Ahmad, al-Baihaqi, al-Hakim, and Ibn Khuzaimah who called it *sahih*.

The Hanafiyyah, Shaf'iyyah, and Hanbaliyyah say it is disliked to fast on Saturday by itself due to the preceding evidence. Malik differs from them, but the *hadith* is proof against him.

(5) It is forbidden to fast on the "day of doubt": 'Ammar ibn Yasir said: "Whoever fasts the 'day of doubt'[10]has disobeyed Abu al-Qasim [the Prophet]." This is related by an-Nasa'i, at-Tirmidhi, Abu Dawud, and Ibn Majah.

Of its status, at-Tirmidhi says: "It is a *hassan sahih hadith*. Most of the knowledgeable people act in accordance with it. It is the opinion of Sufyan ath-Thauri, Malik ibn Anas, 'Abdullah ibn al-Mubarak, ash-Shaf'i, Ahmad, and Ishaq. They all hate that one fasts on a 'day of doubt.' Most of them believe that if one fasts on such a day and it turns out to be Ramadan, then that day still has to be made up later. If such a day occurs during one's regular fasting period, then it is permissible to fast on such a day."

As related by "the group," Abu Hurairah reported that the Messenger of Allah said: "Do not precede Ramadan by fasting the

---

[10]For example, this is when the people are in doubt whether it is the last day of Sha'ban or the first day of Ramadan that is, they did not sight the moon, and they fast just to be on the safe side.

day or two before it unless it is a day on which the person usually fasts."

About this *hadith*, at-Tirmidhi says: "The *hadith* is *hassan sahih* and the scholars act in accordance with it. They dislike that a person should hasten Ramadan by fasting on the day before it. If a person usually fasts on a day and 'the day of doubt' occurs on that day, then there is no problem with his fasting on that day, in their opinion."

(6) It is forbidden to fast every day of the year: It is forbidden to do so because there are certain days of the year on which one is not allowed to fast. The Messenger of Allah said: "There is no [reward for] fasting for the one who perpetually fasts." This is related by Ahmad, al-Bukhari, and Muslim.

If one breaks his fast during the days of *'id* and the days of *tashreeq*, then his perpetual fasting would no longer be considered disliked. In his comments on this issue, at-Tirmidhi says: "A group of scholars dislike fasting every day if it includes the *'ids* [*'id al-Fitr*, *'id al-Adha*] and the days of *tashreeq*. If one breaks his fast on those days, his action is no longer disliked, as he is no longer fasting the whole year." The scholars are Malik, ash-Shaf'i, Ahmad, and Ishaq.

The Prophet approved of Hamzah al-Aslami's numerous fasts when he told him: "Fast if you wish and break your fast if you wish." This *hadith* was mentioned earlier.[11]

(7) It is not allowed for a woman to fast while her husband is present except with his permission: The Messenger of Allah forbade a woman to fast if her husband was present until he gave her his permission to do so. Abu Hurairah reported that the Prophet said: "A woman is not to fast [even] for one day while her husband is present except with his permission, unless it is during Ramadan." This is related by Ahmad, al-Bukhari, and Muslim. The scholars have interpreted this prohibition as one of forbiddance, and they allow the husband to end his wife's fasting if she fasted without his permission and he seeks his right [to sex] from her. This is also true,

---

[11]The actual text of the *hadith* is: "Asma related that Hamzah ibn 'Amr al-Aslami was greatly devoted to fasting and once asked the Messenger of Allah if he could fast while on a journey. The Prophet, upon whom be peace, told him: 'Fast if you wish and break your fast if you wish.' " This is related by al-Bukhari and Muslim. J.Z.

obviously, for days other than those of Ramadan in which case she does not need her husband's permission. Similarly, if she fasted without his permission because he was not present, he has the right to end her fast when he returns.

If the husband is sick or incapable of intercourse, it is permissible for the woman to fast without his permission — that is, it is similar to the case of where the husband is not present.

(8) It is prohibited to fast consecutive days without eating at all [al-wisal]: Abu Hurairah reported that the Messenger of Allah, upon whom be peace, said: "Do not perform *al-wisal*." He said that three times and the people said to him: "But you perform *al-wisal*, O Messenger of Allah!" He said: "You are not like me in that matter. I spend the night in such a state that Allah feeds me and gives me to drink. Devote yourselves to the deeds which you can perform." This is related by al-Bukhari and Muslim.

The scholars say this prohibition implies that the act is disliked. Ahmad and Ishaq say that it is allowed to fast until the time of the pre-dawn meal as long as it is not a hardship on the one fasting. This opinion is based on what al-Bukhari recorded on the authority of Abu Sa'id al-Khudri: "The Messenger of Allah said: 'Do not make *al-wisal*. If one of you insists on making *al-wisal*, he may continue his fast [after sunset] until the time of the pre-dawn meal.'"

Voluntary Fasts

The Prophet has exhorted us to fast during the following days:

Six days of the month of Shawwal: Abu Ayyub al-Ansari reported that the Prophet, upon whom be peace, said: "Whoever fasts during the month of Ramadan and then follows it with six days of Shawwal will be [rewarded] as if he had fasted the entire year." This is related by "the group," except for al-Bukhari and an-Nasa'i.

According to Ahmad, one may fast on these days consecutively or nonconsecutively, as neither practice is preferred over the other. Hanafiyyah and Shafi'iyyah maintain that it is preferable to fast on consecutive days after the 'id.

The first ten days of Dhul-Hijjah, especially the day of Arafah, for those who are not performing the pilgrimage:

(1) Abu Qatadah reported that the Messenger of Allah said: "Fasting on the day of 'Arafah is an expiation for two years, the year preceding it and the year following it. Fasting the day of 'Ashurah is an expiation for the year preceding it." This is related by "the group," except for al-Bukhari and at-Tirmidhi.

(2) Hafsah reported: "There are five things that the Prophet never abandoned: fasting the day of 'Ashurah, fasting the [first] ten [days of Dhul-Hijjah], fasting three days of every month and praying two *rak'ah* before the dawn prayer." This is related by Ahmad and an-Nasa'i.

(3) 'Uqbah ibn 'Amr reported that the Messenger of Allah said: "The day of 'Arafah, the day of sacrifice, and the days of *tashreeq* are *'ids* for us — the people of Islam — and they are days of eating and drinking." This is related by "the five," except for Ibn Majah. At-Tirmidhi grades it *sahih*.

(4) Abu Hurairah stated: "The Messenger of Allah forbade fasting on the day of 'Arafah for one who is actually at 'Arafah." This is related by Ahmad, Abu Dawud, an-Nasa'i, and Ibn Majah.

At-Tirmidhi comments: "The scholars prefer that the day of 'Arafah be fasted unless one is actually at 'Arafah."

(5) Umm al-Fadl said: "The people were in doubt over whether or not the Prophet was fasting on the day of 'Arafah. I sent him some milk, and he drank it while he was delivering an address to the people at 'Arafah." This is related by al-Bukhari and Muslim.

Fasting during the month of Muharram, especially the day of 'Ashurah and the days immediately preceding and following it: Abu Hurairah reported: "I asked the Prophet: 'Which prayer is the best after the obligatory prayers?' He said: 'Prayer during the middle of the night.' I asked: 'Which fast is the best after the fast of Ramadan?' He said, 'The month of Allah that you call Muharram.'" This is related by Ahmad, Muslim, and Abu Dawud.

Mu'awiyyah ibn Abu Sufyan reported that he heard the Messenger of Allah say: "Concerning the day of 'Ashurah, it is not obligatory upon you to fast on it as I do. Whoever wishes may fast and whoever does not wish to is not obliged to do so." This is related by al-Bukhari and Muslim.

'Aishah stated: "The tribe of Quraish used to fast on the day of 'Ashurah in the days before Islam, as did the Prophet. When he came to Madinah, he still fasted on it and ordered the people to do likewise. Then, when fasting during the month of Ramadan became obligatory, he said: 'Whoever wishes may fast ['Ashurah] and whoever wishes may leave it." This is related by al-Bukhari and Muslim.

Ibn 'Abbas reported: "The Prophet came to Madinah and found the Jews fasting on the day of 'Ashurah. He said to them: 'What is this fast?' They said: 'A great day. Allah saved Moses and the tribes of Israel from their enemies on this day and therefore, Moses fasted on this day.' The Prophet said: 'We have more of a right to Moses than you,' so he fasted on that day also and ordered the people to fast on that day." This is recorded by al-Bukhari and Muslim.

According to al-Bukhari and Muslim, Musa al-Ash'ari reported: "The Jews would honor the day of 'Ashurah as an 'id. The Prophet said: 'You [Muslims] are to fast on it.' "

Ibn 'Abbas reported: "The Messenger of Allah fasted on the day of 'Ashurah and ordered the people to fast on it. The people said: 'O Messenger of Allah, it is a day that the Jews and Christians honor.' The Prophet said, 'When the following year comes – Allah willing – we shall fast on the ninth.' The death of the Prophet came before the following year." This is recorded by Muslim and Abu Dawud. In one version the wording is: "If I remain until next year, we shall fast the ninth," meaning, the tenth. This is related by Muslim and Abu Dawud.

The scholars have mentioned that the fast of 'Ashurah is of three levels: (1) fasting three days – that is, on the 9th, 10th, and 11th of Muharram; (2) fasting on the 9th and 10th; and (c) fasting only on the 10th.

Being generous in providing household provisions on the day of 'Arafah: Jabir reported that the Messenger of Allah said: "Whoever is generous to himself and to his family on the day of 'Ashurah will have Allah's generosity bestowed on him for the rest of the year." This is related by al-Baihaqi in *ash-Shu'ab* and by Ibn 'Abdul-Barr. The *hadith* has other chains, but they are all weak; however, strung together these chains strengthen the rank of the *hadith*, as as-Sakhawi said.[12]

---

[12]Ibn Taimiyyah has stated that this *hadith* is fabricated because its meaning is not supported by experience. Most *hadith* scholars, such as al-Baihaqi, al-Albani and so on declare it to be weak, as all of its chains are weak. Al-'Aqiliy also mentions that there is nothing confirmed from the Prophet on this question, and Dr. 'Abdul Muaty Ameen Qalajy did not make any comment upon it. Cf. *Kitab adh-Dhuafa al-Kabeer* (Dar al-Baz, Makkah), vol. 3, p. 252. J.Z.

Fasting most of the month of Sha'ban (the month preceding Ramadan): The Prophet would fast most of the month of Sha'ban. 'Aishah said: "I never saw the Messenger of Allah fast a complete month save for Ramadan, and I have never seen him fast more in a month than he did in Sha'ban." This is related by al-Bukhari and Muslim.

Usamah ibn Zaid inquired: "O Messenger of Allah, I never find you fasting in any month like you do during the month of Sha'ban." The Prophet responded: "That is a month the people neglect. It comes between Rajab and Ramadan. It is a month in which the deeds are raised to the Lord of the Worlds. I love that my deeds be raised while I am fasting." This is related by Abu Dawud, an-Nasa'i, and by Ibn Khuzaimah in his *Sahih*.

Some people fast on the 15th of Sha'ban in particular, thinking that that day contains more virtues than the other days. This is an unsubstantiated claim.

Fasting during the "forbidden" months: The "forbidden" months (during which killing is forbidden) are Dhul-Qidah, Dhul-Hijjah, Muharram, and Rajab. It is preferred to fast a lot during these months.

A man from Bahila came to the Prophet and said: "O Messenger of Allah, I am the man who came to you during the first year." The Prophet, upon whom be peace, said: "What has changed you? You used to be much more handsome!" He answered: "I did not eat save during the night since I left you." The Messenger of Allah asked: "Why did you punish yourself? Fast during the month of patience [that is, Ramadan] and then one day of every month." The man said: "Add something to that for me, for I have more strength than that." The Prophet responded: "Fast two days [a month]." The man said: "Add more for me." The Prophet said three times: "Fast from the forbidden months, then leave fasting." He pointed with three of his fingers by clenching them and releasing them.[13] This is related by Ahmad, Abu Dawud, Ibn Majah, and al-Baihaqi with a good chain.

Fasting during Rajab contains no more virtue than during any other month. There is no sound report from the *sunnah* that states that it has a special reward. All that has been related concerning it

---

[13]He was alluding to the fact that the person should fast for three days and then refrain fasting for three days, and so on.

is not strong enough to be used as a proof. Ibn Hajr says: "There is no authentic *hadith* related to its virtues, not fasting during it or on certain days of it, nor concerning exclusively making night prayers during that month."

Fasting Mondays and Thursdays: Abu Hurairah reported that the most the Prophet would fast would be Monday and Thursday. He was asked about that and he said: "The actions are presented on every Monday and Thursday. Allah forgives every Muslim or every believer, except for those who are boycotting each other. He says [about them]: 'Leave them.' " This is related by Ahmad with a *sahih* chain. It is recorded in *Sahih Muslim* that the Prophet, when asked about fasting on Monday, said: "That is the day on which I was born and the day on which I received revelations."

Fasting three days of every month: Abu Dharr al-Ghafari reported: "The Messenger of Allah ordered us to fast for three days of every month — that is, on the days of the full moon (the 13th, 14th, and 15th of the lunar month). And he said: 'It is like fasting the whole year.' " This is related by an-Nasa'i and by Ibn Hibban, who called it *sahih*.

It is related that the Prophet would fast on Saturday, Sunday, and Monday of one month and on Tuesday, Wednesday, and Thursday of the next month. He would also fast for three days at the beginning of the month, or on the first Thursday and the next two Mondays of the month.

Fasting one day and not fasting the next: Abu Salama ibn 'Abdurrahman reported from 'Abdullah ibn 'Amr that the Prophet, upon whom be peace, said to him: 'I have been informed that you stay up in prayer during the night and fast during the day. 'Abdullah answered: "Yes, O Messenger of Allah." The Prophet said: "Fast and do not fast, pray and sleep, for your body, your wife, and your guests have a right upon you. It is sufficient for you to fast three days a month." 'Abdullah said: "I wanted to be stricter on myself and I said: "O Messenger of Allah, I have the strength to do more." The Prophet said: "Then fast three days a week." 'Abdullah said: "I have the strength to do more!" The Prophet said: "Fast the fast of the Prophet David and do not do more than that!" 'Abdullah inquired: "And what was the fast of David?" The Prophet replied: "He would fast one day and then not fast the next." This is recorded by Ahmad and others.

Ahmad also related from 'Abdullah ibn 'Amr that the Prophet said: "The fast most loved by Allah is the fast of David, and the most loved prayer is the prayer of David. He would sleep half the night, pray for a third of the night, and then sleep during the last sixth of the night. He would also fast one day and then eat on the next."

It is permissible for one who is performing a voluntary fast to break his fast: Umm Hani reported that the Prophet, upon whom be peace, entered her room during the day of the conquest of Makkah. He was offered something to drink and he drank from it. Then he offered it to Umm Hani and she said: "I am fasting." The Prophet said: "The one who is fasting voluntarily is in charge of himself. If you wish you may fast and if you wish you may break your fast." This is recounted by Ahmad, ad-Daraqutni, and al-Baihaqi. Al-Hakim also related it and said that its chain is *sahih.* The version he recorded states: "And if one wishes he may fast and if he wishes he may break his fast."

Abu Juhaifah said: "The Prophet established the bond of brotherhood between Salman and Abu ad-Darda. Once, Salman visited Abu ad-Darda and saw Umm ad-Darda wearing very plain clothes. He said to her: 'What's happening to you?' She said: 'Your brother Abu ad-Darda has no need in this world.' When Abu ad-Darda came, he prepared some food for Salman and said: 'Eat, for I am fasting.' Salman said: 'I shall not eat until you eat.' So he ate. When it was night, Abu ad-Darda got up to pray and Salman said, 'Sleep,' and he did so. Toward the end of the night Salman woke Abu ad-Darda and said, Pray now.' And they prayed. Salman told him: 'Your Lord has a right upon you, you have a right upon yourself, and so does your wife. Give each one its due right.' Abu ad-Darda went to the Prophet and told him what Salman had said. The Prophet said: 'Salman has said the truth.' " This is related by al-Bukhari and at-Tirmidhi.

Abu Sa'id al-Khudri said: "I prepared food for the Prophet. He came to me with some of his companions. When the food was laid out, one of the men said: 'I am fasting.' The Messenger of Allah said: 'Your brother has invited you and incurred expenses in your behalf.' Then he asked [him], Break your fast and fast another day in its place if you wish.' " This is related by al-Baihaqi. Al-Hafidh says it has a *hassan* chain.

Most scholars maintain that one who is performing a voluntary fast can break it. It is, however, preferred to make up that day later on. The preceding view is clear and authentic *ahadith* are support for that position.

The Manners of Fasting

It is preferred for the fasting person to observe the following manners:

(1) Eating a pre-dawn meal: All Muslims agree that it is preferred to eat a pre-dawn meal and that there is no sin upon one who does not do so. Anas reported that the Messenger of Allah said: "Eat a pre-dawn meal, for there are blessings in it." This is related by al-Bukhari and Muslim.

Al-Miqdām ibn Madyakrib reported that the Prophet, upon whom be peace, said: "You should eat this pre-dawn meal for it is a blessed nourishment." This is related by an-Nasa'i with a good chain. The reason why it is a blessing is that it strengthens the fasting person, makes him more energetic, and makes the fast easier for him.

(a) What would fulfill the *sunnah* of eating a pre-dawn meal: The *sunnah* would be fulfilled by eating a small or large quantity of food, or even just by drinking a sip of water. Abu Sa'id al-Khudri reported that the Messenger of Allah said: "The pre-dawn meal is blessed, so do not neglect it even if you only take a sip of water. Verily, Allah and the angels pray for those who have pre-dawn meals." This is related by Ahmad.

(b) The time for the pre-dawn meal: The time for the pre-dawn meal is between the middle of the night and dawn. It is considered best to delay it (that is, as close to dawn a possible). Zaid ibn Thabit reported: "We ate the pre-dawn meal with the Messenger of Allah and then we got up for the prayer. He was asked: 'What was the amount of time between the two?' He responded: '[The time it would take to recite] fifty verses.'" This is recounted by al-Bukhari and Muslim.

'Amr ibn Maimun adds: "The companions of Muhammad, upon whom be peace, would be the first to break the fast and the last to eat their pre-dawn meals." This is recorded by al-Baihaqi with a *sahih* chain.

Abu Dharr al-Ghafari related that the Prophet said: "My nation will always retain some goodness as long as they hasten breaking the fast and delay eating the pre-dawn meal." This *hadith* has in its chain one Sulaim ibn Abu Uthman who is unknown.[14]

(c) **Doubt concerning the time of** *fajr*: If one is in doubt whether or not the time of *fajr* has begun or not, he may continue to eat and drink until he is certain that it is *fajr*. He should not base his action on doubt or suspicion. Allah has made the signs for beginning the daily fast very clear and unambiguous. Allah enjoins (upon the believers) in the Qur'an: "Eat and drink until the white thread of the dawn becomes distinct from the black thread [of the night]."

A man said to Ibn 'Abbas: "I eat until I suspect that its time has ended so I stop. Ibn 'Abbas observed: "Continue to eat until you are certain about the time." Abu Dawud reported that Ahmad ibn Hanbal said: "If you have some doubt about *fajr*, eat until you are sure dawn has come." This is the opinion of Ibn 'Abbas, 'Ata, al-'Auza'i, and Ahmad.,

An-Nawawi informs that: "The followers of ash-Shaf'i agree that one may eat if he is uncertain whether dawn has come or not."

(2) **Hastening in breaking the fast:** It is preferred for the fasting person to hasten in breaking the fast when the sun has set. Sahl ibn Sad reported that the Prophet said: "The people will always be with the good as long as they hasten in breaking the fast." This is related by al-Bukhari and Muslim.

The fast should be broken with an odd number of dates or, if that is not available, with some water. Anas reported: "The Messenger of Allah would break his fast with ripe dates before he would pray. If those were not available, he would eat dried dates. If those were not available, he would drink some water." This *hadith* is related by Abu Dawud and by al-Hakim, who called it *sahih*, and by at-Tirmidhi, who called it *hassan*.

Sulaiman ibn 'Amr reported that the Prophet said: "If one of you is fasting, he should break his fast with dates. If dates are not available, then with water, for water is purifying." This is related by Ahmad and by at-Tirmidhi, who called it *hassan sahih*.

The preceding *hadith* also shows that it is preferred to break the fast in the above manner before praying. After the prayer, the person may continue to eat, but if the evening meal is ready, one may begin with that. Anas reported that the Messenger of Allah

---

[14]The *hadith* is weak and therefore should have been deleted. J.Z.

said: "If the food is already presented, eat before the sunset prayer and do not eat your meals in haste." This is related by al-Bukhari and Muslim.

(3) Supplications while breaking the fast and while fasting: Ibn Majah related from 'Abdullah ibn 'Amr ibn al-'Aas that the Prophet, upon whom be peace, said: "A fasting person, upon break-ing his fast, has a supplication that will not be rejected.[15] When 'Abdullah broke his fast he would say: "O Allah, I ask of You, by Your mercy that encompasses everything, to forgive me."

It is confirmed that the Prophet would say: The thirst has gone, the glands are wet and, Allah willing, the reward is confirmed. In *mursal* form, it is reported that he would say: "O Allah, for You I have fasted and with Your provisions do I break my fast."

At-Tirmidhi recorded, with a good chain, that the Prophet said: "Three people will not have their supplications rejected: a fasting person until he breaks his fast, a just ruler, and an oppressed person."

(4) Refraining from performing any actions that do not befit the fasting: Fasting is a type of worship that draws one closer to Allah. Allah has prescribed it to purify the soul and to train it in good deeds. The fasting person must be on guard against any act that may cause him to lose the benefits of his fast. Thus, his fast will increase his God-consciousness, and Allah says in the Qur'an: "O you who believe, fasting is prescribed for you as it was prescribed for those before you so perchance you may attain God-consciousness."

Fasting is not just refraining from eating and drinking, but it is also refraining from everything else that Allah has forbidden. Abu Hurairah reported that the Prophet said: "Fasting is not [abstaining] from eating and drinking only, but also from vain speech and foul language. If one of you is being cursed or annoyed, he should say: "I am fasting, I am fasting." This is related by Ibn Khuzaimah, Ibn Hibban, and al-Hakim. The latter said that it is *sahih* according to Muslim's criterion.

Abu Hurairah also reported that the Prophet, upon whom be peace, said: "Allah does not need the fast of one who does not aban-

---

[15]This *hadith* is weak.

don false speech or acting according to his false speech." This is related by the group, except for Muslim.

Abu Hurairah narrated that the Prophet said: "Perhaps a fasting person will get nothing from his fast save hunger, and perhaps the one who stands to pray at night will get nothing from his standing except sleeplessness." This is related by an-Nasa'i, Ibn Majah, and al-Hakim. The latter said that it is *sahih* according to al-Bukhari's criterion.

(5) Using the tooth stick [brush]: It is preferred for the fasting person to use a tooth stick or a brush. There is no difference if he uses it at the beginning or the ending of the day. At-Tirmidhi affirms that: "Ash-Shafhi did not see anything wrong with using a tooth stick [brush] during the beginning or the ending of the day." The Prophet would use his tooth stick [brush] while fasting.

(6) Being generous and studying the Qur'an: Being generous and studying the Qur'an is recommended during any time, but it is especially stressed during the month of Ramadan. Al-Bukhari recorded that Ibn 'Abbas said: "The Prophet was the most generous of people, but he would be his most generous during Ramadan when he would meet with [the angel] Gabriel. He would meet with him every night and recite the Qur'an. When Gabriel met him, he used to be more generous than a fast wind."

(7) Striving to perform as many acts of worship as possible during the last ten days of Ramadan: Al-Bukhari and Muslim record from 'Aishah that during the last ten days of Ramadan, the Messenger of Allah would wake his wives up during the night and then remain apart from them (that is, being busy in acts of worship). A version in Muslim states: "He would strive [to do acts of worship] during the last ten days of Ramadan more than he would at any other time." At-Tirmidhi also recorded this from 'Ali.

Acts That are Permissible During the Fast

The following acts are permissible for the fasting person:

(1) Pouring water over one's self and submersing one's self in water: Abu Bakr ibn 'Abdurrahman reported from a number of companions that they had seen Allah's Messenger pour water over his head while he was fasting due to thirst or extreme heat. This is related by Ahmad, Malik, and Abu Dawud with a *sahih* chain.

In the two *Sahih* of al-Bukhari and Muslim, it is related from 'Aishah that the Prophet would rise in the morning on a fasting day and then would perform *ghusl* (a complete bath). If during the bath some water is swallowed unintentionally, the fast is still valid.

(2) Applying *kohl* or eyedrops or anything else to the eyes: These acts are all permissible, even if some taste from it finds its way to the throat, as the eyes are not a passageway to the stomach. Anas reported that he would apply *kohl* while he was fasting. This is the opinion of the Shaf'iyyah. Ibn al-Mundhir records the same opinion from 'Ata, al-Hassan, an-Nakha'i, al-Auza'i, Abu Hanifah, Abu Thaur, and Dawud. It is related from the following companions: Ibn 'Umar, Anas, and Ibn Abu 'Aufa. According to at-Tirmidhi, nothing authentic has been related from the Prophet concerning this question.

(3) Kissing for one who has the ability to control himself: It is confirmed that 'Aishah said: "The Prophet would kiss and embrace while he was fasting, for he had the most control of all of you over his desires." 'Umar said: "I was excited one time and I kissed [my wife] while I was fasting. I went to the Prophet and said: 'Today I committed a horrendous act — I kissed while I was fasting.' The Prophet asked: 'What do you think of rinsing with water while fasting?' I said: 'There is nothing wrong with that.' The Prophet said: 'Then what is the question about?' "

Ibn al-Mundhir says: " 'Umar, Ibn 'Abbas, Abu Hurairah, 'Aishah, 'Ata, ash-Sha'bi, al-Hassan, Ahmad, and Ishaq permit kissing. The Hanafiyyah and Shaf'iyyah say that it is disliked if it incites one's desires. If it does not do so, it is not disliked although it is better to avoid it." There is no difference between an old man or a young man in this matter. The question is whether or not the kiss excites one's desires. If it does, it is disliked. If it does not, it is not disliked although it is best to avoid it. It does not matter if the kiss was on the cheek or on the lips, and so on. Touching with the hand or embracing follow the same ruling as kissing.

(4) Any type of injection: Injections do not break the fast whether they are for feeding the person or just medicine. It does not matter if the injection was intraveinous or underneath the skin. It also does not matter if what was injected reaches the stomach, as it does not reach the stomach through the customary manner (that food does).

(5) Cupping to drain blood: The Prophet, upon whom be peace, was cupped while he was fasting. However, if doing this weakens the fasting person, it is disliked. Thabit al-Bunani asked Anas: "Did you dislike cupping for a fasting person during the time of the Prophet?" He answered: "No [we did not], unless it made someone weak." This is related by al-Bukhari and others. Vivisection follows the same ruling as cupping.

(6) Rinsing the mouth and nose: These acts are allowed in general, but it is disliked to exaggerate (that is, use a lot of water and put the water deep into the mouth or nose while fasting). Laqit ibn Sabra reported that the Prophet said: "Exaggerate when rinsing your nose unless you are fasting." This is related by an-Nasa'i, Abu Dawud, at-Tirmidhi, and Ibn Majah. At-Tirmidhi called it *hassan sahih*.

Scholars dislike using nose drops (that is, applying medicine through the nose) while one is fasting, for they are of the opinion that it breaks the fast. There is a *hadith* that supports their opinion.

Ibn Qudamah sums up the various opinions on the subject: "If while gargling or rinsing the nose for the sake of purifying one's self [for example, for prayer] water reaches the throat unintentionally and not due to exaggeration, there is no problem. This is according to al-Auza'i, Ishaq, and one statement from ash-Shaf'i, which is related from Ibn 'Abbas. Malik and Abu Hanifah hold that it breaks the fast because that water reaches the stomach. If he was aware that he was fasting, it breaks his fast, as if he would have drunk intentionally. The first opinion is stronger, since [the water] reached the throat without intention or exaggeration. It is similar to having a fly enter the mouth and proceed to the throat. That differentiates it from an intentional act."

(7) Those things which one could not protect one's self from, such as swallowing one's saliva, the dust of the road, sifting flour and so on are all overlooked: Ibn 'Abbas ruling is that: "There is no problem with tasting liquid food or something you wish to purchase." Al-Hassan used to chew the walnuts for his grandson while he was fasting. Ibrahim also permitted that.

Chewing gum (unlike the one in vogue in the West, it has no sweetness or fragrance) is disliked. The gum must not break into pieces. Those who say that it is disliked include ash-Sha'bi, an-Nakha'i, the Hanafiyyah, the Shaf'iyyah, and the Hanbaliyyah. 'Aishah and 'Ata permit chewing, as nothing reaches the stomach and it is just like putting pebbles into one's mouth provided it does not break into parts. If a part of it breaks off and enters the stomach, it will break the fast.

Ibn Taimiyyah says: "Smelling perfumes does not harm the fast." Enlarging upon the subject, he says: "As for *kohl*, injections, drops dropped into the urethra [that is, enemas for medicinal purposes], and treatment for brain and stomach injuries, there is some dispute among the scholars. Some say that none of these break the fast, some say that all except *kohl* would break the fast, while others say all except the drops break the fast, or that the *kohl* or drops do not break the fast but that the rest do." Ibn Taimiyyah continues: "The first opinion on this question is preferred. The most apparent conclusion is that none of them break the fast. The fast is part of the religion of Islam. Both the layman and specialist must be knowledgeable about it. If the preceding actions were forbidden by Allah and His Messenger to the fasting person because they would ruin the fast, then it would have been obligatory upon the Messenger to clarify that fact. If he had done so, his companions would have known about it and would have passed it on to the rest of the Muslims. Since no one has related that not from the Prophet, not with an authentic or a weak *hadith*, nor in *mursal* or *musnad* form then it must be the case that such acts do not void [the fast]." He also says: "If the ruling is one that would affect everyone or everyday matters, then the Prophet would have clarified it to a general audience. It is well-known that *kohl* was in common use as were oils, washing, incense, and perfume. If they broke the fast, the Prophet would have mentioned them, as he mentioned other things [that break the fast]. Since he did not do so, they belong to the class of perfumes, incense, and dyes. Incense goes through the nose and enters the head and lands on the body. Dyes or oils are absorbed by the skin and the body is refreshened by it. The case of perfumes is similar. Since these have not been [explicitly] prohibited to the fasting person, it points to the fact that using them is permissible for the fasting person and so is *kohl*. The Muslims during the time of the Prophet would injure themselves, either from *jihad* or otherwise, and would injure their stomachs or skulls. If that would have ended their fasts, it would have been made clear to them [by the Prophet].

Since that was not prohibited for the fasting person, it must not break the fast." Ibn Taimiyyah continues: "No one eats *kohl* and no one causes it to enter his stomach — neither through his nose nor through his mouth. Anal enemas are also not taken as food. Indeed, it helps the body to release whatever is in the intestines and it does not reach the stomach. Any medicine that is used to treat stomach wounds or head injuries [that is taken orally] is not considered similar to food. Allah says in the Qur'an: 'Fasting is prescribed for you as it was prescribed for those before you.' The Prophet, upon whom be peace, said: 'Fasting is a shield,' and, Verily, Satan rushes through the body like the flowing of the blood [in the body]. You should constrict his rushing by hunger and fasting.'[16] To increase his Allah-consciousness a fasting person must not eat or drink because food and drink cause the veins to fill up with blood in which Satan circulates [in one's body]. They become easier for Satan through eating and drinking, not from enemas, *kohl*, or medicines applied through the penis or used to treat stomach and brain injuries."

(8) The fasting person can eat, drink, and perform sexual intercourse until *fajr*: If someone has food in his mouth when *fajr* is beginning, he should spit it out. If he is having intercourse (with his wife) at that time, he should immediately stop. If he does so, his fast will still be valid. If he continues in these actions at that time, he will have broken his fast. Al-Bukhari and Muslim record from Aishah that the Prophet said: "Bilal makes the call to prayer while it is still night; therefore, eat and drink until Ibn Umm Maktum makes the call to prayer."

(9) It is permissible for the fasting person to be sexually defiled in the morning (that is, a person is not required to perform *ghusl* before *fajr*): The *hadith* from 'Aishah on this point has already been mentioned.

(10) Menstruating or post-childbirth bleeding women: If the blood of a menstruating woman or of a woman with post-childbirth bleeding stops during the night, she can delay *ghusl* until the morn-

---

[16]Al-Albani noted, in his edition of Ibn Taimiyyah's book on fasting, that the additional words "You should constrict . . ." have no source in any *hadith* of the Prophet. J.Z.

ing and still fast but, she must perform *ghusl* before the morning prayer.

Actions that Void the Fast

The actions that void the fast may be divided into two types: (a) those which void the fast and require that the day be made up later, and (b) those which void the fast and, in addition to being made up, also require an act of expiation.

Category (a) is made up of the following acts:

Intentional eating or drinking: If one eats due to forgetfulness, a mistake, or coercion, then he does not have to make up the day later or perform any expiation. Abu Hurairah reported that the Prophet said: "Whoever forgets he is fasting, and eats or drinks is to complete his fast, as it was Allah who fed him and gave him something to drink." This is related by the group.

Commenting on it, at-Tirmidhi says: "Most of the scholars act according to this *hadith*. It is the opinion of Sufyan ath-Thauri, ash-Shaf'i, Ahmad, and Ishaq."

Abu Hanifah reported that the Prophet said: "Whoever breaks his fast during Ramadan due to forgetfulness is not to make up the day later or to perform any expiation." This is related by ad-Daraqutni, al-Baihaqi, and al-Hakim, who says that it is *sahih* according to Muslim's criterion. Ibn Hajr says that its chain is *sahih*.

Ibn 'Abbas reported that the Prophet said: "Allah will not hold anyone of this nation responsible for what is done in error, forgetfulness or under coercion." This is recounted by Ibn Majah, at-Tabarani, and al-Hakim.

Intentional vomiting: If one is overcome and vomits unintentionally, he does not have to make up the day later on or perform the acts of expiation. Abu Hurairah reported that the Prophet, upon whom be peace, said: "Whoever is overcome and vomits is not to make up the day." Whoever vomits intentionally must make up the day." This is related by Ahmad, Abu Dawud, at-Tirmidhi, Ibn Majah, Ibn Hibban, ad-Daraqutni, and al-Hakim. The latter called it *sahih*.

Of the report's credibility, al-Khattabi says: "I do not know of any difference of opinion among the scholars on this point. If one vomits unintentionally he is not in need of making up the day, while one who vomits intentionally must make up the day later."

The menses and post-childbirth bleeding: Even if such bleeding begins just before the sunset, the fast of that day is rendered void and the day must be made up. There is a consensus of scholars on this point.

Ejaculation of sperm: Ejaculation voids the fast even if it was just due to kissing, hugging, or masturbation, and the day must be made up. If the ejaculation was due to looking at or thinking about something, then it is like having a wet dream during the day and it, therefore, does not void the fast nor is there any requirement on the person. Similarly, ejaculation of seminal fluid does not harm the fast in any way.

Eating something that is not nourishing, such as salt: Someone who uses a lot of salt for a reason other than eating, in which it goes down to the stomach, breaks the fast according to most scholars.

If one has the intention, while he is fasting, to break the fast, he in effect voids the fast even if he does not actually eat anything: This is because the intention is one of the pillars of the fast and, if one changes his intention, he has nullified his fast.

If one eats, drinks, or has intercourse, thinking that the sun has set or that *fajr* has not occurred: In such cases, according to most scholars and the four *imams*, that person is to make up that day. However, there is a difference of opinion on this point. Ishaq, Dawud, Ibn Hazm, 'Ata, 'Urwah, al-Hassan al-Basri, and Mujahid maintain that such a fast is sound and that the person need not make up the day later. They base their opinion on the fact that Allah says in the Qur'an: "And there is no sin for you in the mistakes you make unintentionally, but what your hearts purpose [that will be a sin for you]."

The Messenger of Allah, upon whom be peace, said: "Allah will not hold anyone of this nation responsible for what is done by mistake ..."

'Abdurrazaq related that Mamar reported from al-Amash that Zaid ibn Wahb said: "The people broke their fast during the time of 'Umar ibn al-Khattab. I saw a big pot being brought from Hafsah's house and the people drank. Then the sun appeared from behind the clouds and this distressed the people. They said: 'We have to make up this day.' 'Umar asked: 'Why? By Allah, we have not involved ourselves in any sin.' "

Al-Bukhari records that Asma' bint Abu Bakr said: "We broke the fast of Ramadan when it was cloudy during the time of the Prophet, and then the sun appeared again."

Commenting on the subject, Ibn Taimiyyah says: "This points to two things: (1) that it is not preferred for one to delay breaking the fast until one is absolutely certain that the sun has set ... and (2) that it is not necessary to make up such a day. If the Prophet would have ordered them to make up that day, it would have become public knowledge. The fact that it has been related that they broke their fast [and that it has not been related that they were ordered to make up that day] points to the fact that they were not ordered to make up that day."

The only action, according to most scholars, which requires that both the day be made up and the act of expiation be performed is having sexual intercourse during a day of Ramadan.

Abu Hurairah reported that a man came to the Messenger of Allah and said: "I am destroyed, O Messenger of Allah!" The Prophet asked: "What has destroyed you?" He said, "I had intercourse with my wife during a day of Ramadan." The Prophet asked: "Are you able to free a slave?" He said, "No". The Prophet asked: "Is it possible for you to fast for two consecutive months?" He said, "No." The Prophet asked: "Is it possible for you to feed sixty poor people?" He said, "No." The Prophet said: "Then sit." A basket of dates was brought to the Prophet and he said to the man: Give this in charity. The man said: "To someone poorer than us? There is no one in this city who is poorer than us!" The Prophet laughed until his molar teeth could be seen and said: "Go and feed your family with it." This is related by the group.[17]

Most scholars say that both men and women have to perform the acts of expiation if they intentionally have intercourse during a day of Ramadan[18] on which they had intended to fast. If they had intercourse out of forgetfulness or not due to choice — that is, due to coercion, or they did not have the intention to fast, then the expia-

---

[17]This *hadith* is used as a proof by those who say that the expiation is not to be offered if it would place a great burden on someone. This is the opinion of ash-Shaf'i. The Hanbaliyyah and some of the Malikiyyah also subscribe to it. Most scholars say that the expiation is to be performed even if it causes the person hardship. Sabiq's footnote.

[18]If they had sexual intercourse on a day being fasted to make up for a day missed during Ramadan, or due to an oath, no expiation is required. Sabiq's footnote.

tion is not obligatory on either one of them. If the woman was forced to have intercourse by the man, the expiation will be obligatory only upon the man.

According to ash-Shaf'i, the expiation is not obligatory upon the woman in any case — that is, regardless if it was due to choice or coercion, and she need only make up the day of fasting that she voided. An-Nawawi says: "The most authentic opinion, in general, is that the expiation is obligatory upon the man only and that there is nothing upon the woman. There is nothing obligatory on her in relation to this matter, as it is a matter of [paying] money [due to something related to] sexual intercourse and this refers to the duty of the man and not the woman. [In this way,] it is similar to the case of dowry."

Abu Dawud says: "Ahmad was asked about someone who had sex during Ramadan: 'Is there any expiation upon the woman?' He said: 'I have not heard of any.'" In *al-Mughni* it is stated: "This refers to the fact that the Prophet ordered the man who had had sexual intercourse to free a slave. He did not order the woman to do anything, although he obviously knew that she was a partner in the act."

According to most scholars, acts of expiation must be performed in the order that was mentioned in the *hadith*. The first command is to free a slave. If this is not possible, the person is to fast for two consecutive months. If that is not possible, the person is to feed sixty poor people with meals that are similar to an average meal in his household. The person cannot jump from one act to another unless he is not able to perform the prior order commanded. According to the Malikiyyah and a narration from Ahmad, the person is free to choose any of the above three acts and that will be sufficient for him.

This latter opinion is based on the report from Malik and Ibn Juraij on the authority of Humaid ibn 'Abdurrahman who reported that Abu Hurairah narrated that a man broke his fast during Ramadan and the Prophet ordered him, as an expiation, to free a slave or fast two months consecutively or to feed sixty poor people. This is related by Muslim.

In the preceding *hadith*, the word "or" implies choice, but according to some, the reason for the expiation to be performed was different and therefore the person could choose, as in the case of the expiation for breaking an oath. Ash-Shaukani says: "In the different narrations, there is evidence that the expiation is to be performed in order or according to one's choice. Those who relate it to be in order

are more in number. Al-Muhallab and al-Qurtubi combined the narrations and said that the event [of someone breaking the fast]
occurred more than once."

Al-Hafidh differs: "This is not correct. It was just one event
and the parts are all united. So the crux of the matter is that there
was not more than one event. Some combine the reports and say
that following the order is preferred, but that one may choose.
Others say the opposite."

Whoever has sexual intercourse (with his wife) on a day of
Ramadan and, before he performs the act of expiation, has intercourse on another day of Ramadan, need only perform one act of
expiation according to a narration from Ahmad and the
Hanafiyyah. This is because there is a punishment for acts that are
repeated, and if the expiation or punishment is not carried out, all
the acts are taken together as one. According to Malik, ash-Shaf'i,
and Ahmad, the person must perform the expiation twice, as each
day of Ramadan is a separate act of worship. If the expiation is
obligatory because the person voided the fast, the separate acts are
not combined together.

All scholars agree that if the person intentionally had intercourse during a day of Ramadan and has performed the expiation
and then has intercourse on another day of Ramadan, then another
expiation becomes obligatory upon him. Similarly, they are in agreement that if one has intercourse twice during a day, before performing the expiation for the first act, then he need only perform one act
of expiation. If he has performed the expiation for the first one, then
he need not perform an act of expiation for the second, according to
most scholars. Ahmad says that in such a case, he must perform a
total of two acts of expiation.

Making Up Missed Days of Ramadan

Making up missed days of Ramadan is an obligation that need
not be fulfilled immediately because the time for fulfilling is very
wide and one may perform it at any time. This is also the case with
the fast of expiation. It has been authentically reported that
'Aishah would make up her missed days during the month of
Sha'ban (the month preceding Ramadan), and that she did not perform them immediately even if she had the ability to do so.

Observing the fast of Ramadan and making up the days are
the same with respect to the fact that if one day of Ramadan is
missed, then only one day needs to be made up. There is no addi-

tional penalty. They differ about the fact that when a person makes up the missed days he need not do so on consecutive days. This is because Allah says: "For him who is sick or on a journey, [the same] number of other days" — that is, whoever is sick or traveling and breaks the fast must fast the same number of days that he missed, consecutively or unconsecutively.

Allah has ordered the fast in a general manner without any restricting clauses.

As for making up the missed days of Ramadan, ad-Daraqutni recorded from Ibn 'Umar that the Prophet said: "If you wish, make them on nonconsecutive days and if you wish on consecutive days."

If one delays performing the missed days of fasting until the next Ramadan comes, he is to fast the present Ramadan and then make up the days from the previous Ramadan. There is no ransom payment to be made, regardless of whether the person delayed the fasting due to some acceptable excuse or not. This is the opinion of the Hanafiyyah and al-Hassan al-Basri. Malik, ash-Shaf'i, Ahmad, and Ishaq agree that there is no ransom payment if the fasting was delayed due to some excuse, but they differ when the fasting was delayed without any acceptable excuse. In such a case, according to them, the person should fast the present Ramadan and then make up the days he missed from the previous Ramadan along with a ransom payment of a *madd* of food given in charity each day. It should be noted that they have no acceptable evidence for that opinion. Apparently, the correct opinion is that of the Hanafiyyah, as there is no lawmaking without an authentic legal text to support it (that is, a Qur'anic verse or *hadith*).[19]

Whoever dies and still had some days of Ramadan to make up: The scholars agree that if an individual dies and has missed some prayers during his life, his guardian or heir is not to perform those prayers on his behalf. Similarly, if one does not have the ability to fast, no one is to fast for him while he is alive. There is a difference of opinion over the case of one who dies and has not made up some days of fasting although he had the ability to do so.

---

[19]Similarly, there is no evidence for the ruling that I have often heard in the United States which describes, that is, if the person did not make up the missed days of Ramadan until the next Ramadan, he has to fast two days for every day that he missed. J.Z.

Most scholars, including Abu Hanifah, Malik, and the Shaf'iyyah, say that the guardian or heir is not to fast on such a person's behalf, but is to feed one person a day for the missed days. The chosen opinion, however, among the Shaf'iyyah is that it is preferred for the guardian to fast on the deceased's behalf, thus fulfilling his duty. There is therefore no need for him to feed anyone.

The meaning of guardian is near relative, whether it be an agnate or an heir or someone else. If a non-relative fasts for the deceased, it will only be valid if he got the permission of the guardian.

The proof for the preceding is what Ahmad, al-Bukhari, and Muslim recorded from 'Aishah. The Messenger of Allah, upon whom be peace, said: "If one dies and has some fasts to make up, then his guardian' should fast on his behalf." Al-Bazzar added the words: "If he wishes to do so, while Ibn 'Abbas related that a man came to the Prophet and said: "O Messenger of Allah, my mother died and a month's fasting was due from her. Should I fast on her behalf?" The Prophet asked: "If your mother had a debt would you fulfill it for her?" He said, "Yes." The Prophet observed: "A debt to Allah has more of a right to be fulfilled." This is related by Ahmad, at-Tirmidhi, an-Nasa'i, Abu Dawud, and Ibn Majah.

An-Nawawi [one of the most knowledgeable of the Shaf'iyyah] says: "That statement is the most authentic one, and we follow it. This is the opinion that has been determined to be correct according to our companions in both *hadith* and *fiqh*."

Places where the day is extremely long and the night is short: Scholars differ about what the Muslims who are in areas where the day is extremely long and the night is short should do. What timings should they follow? Some say they should follow the norms of the areas where the Islamic legislation took place — that is, Makkah or Madinah. Others say they should follow the timings of the area that is closest to them which has normal days and nights.

The Night of *Qadr*

Its virtue: The night of *qadr* is the most virtuous night of the year. Allah says in the Qur'an: "We revealed it on the night of power [that is, *qadr*]. What will tell you what the night of power is? It is better than a thousand months." Any action therein, for example, reciting the Qur'an, making remembrance of Allah, and so on, is better than acting for one thousand months which do not contain the night of *qadr*.

It is preferred to seek this night: It is preferred to seek this night during the last ten nights of Ramadan, as the Prophet, upon whom be peace, strove his best in seeking it during that time. We have already mentioned that the Prophet would stay up during the last ten nights, would wake his wives, and then would remain apart from them to worship.

Which night is it?: Scholars hold different opinions as to the night which is the night of *qadr*. Some are of the opinion that it is the 21st, some say the 23rd, others say the 25th and still others say it is the 29th. Some say that it varies from year to year but it is always among the last ten nights of Ramadan. Most scholars, though, vouch for the 27th.

Ahmad recorded, with a *sahih* chain, from Ibn 'Umar that the Prophet said: "He who likes to seek that night should do so on the 27th. Ubayy ibn K'ab said: By Allah, and there is no God but Him, it is during Ramadan — and He swore to that — and by Allah, I know what night it is. It is the night during which the Prophet ordered us to make prayers, the night of the 27th. Its sign is that the sun rises in the morning white and without any rays." This is related by Muslim, Abu Dawud, Ahmad, and by at-Tirmidhi who called it *sahih*.

Praying and making supplications during the night of *qadr*: Al-Bukhari and Muslim record from Abu Hurairah that the Prophet, upon whom be peace, said: "Whoever prays during the night of *qadr* with faith and hoping for its reward will have all of his previous sins forgiven."

As to the supplication during the night of *qadr*, 'Aishah said: "I asked the Messenger of Allah: 'O Messenger of Allah, if I know what night is the night of *qadr*, what should I say during it?' He said: 'Say: O Allah, You are pardoning and You love to pardon, so pardon me.'" This is related by Ahmad, Ibn Majah, and by at-Tirmidhi, who called it *sahih*.

I'TIKĀF OR SECLUSION IN THE MOSQUE

Its meaning: *I'tikaf* means to stick to something, whether good or bad, and to block out everything else. Allah says in the Qur'an: "What then are images that you pay devotion [*akifūn*] to them?" [*al-Anbia'*: 52] — that is, what they devoted themselves to in worship. What is meant here is the seclusion and staying in the mosque with the intention of becoming closer to Allah.

Its legitimacy: All scholars agree on its legitimacy. The Prophet would perform *i'tikāf* for ten days every Ramadan. In the year that he died, he performed it for twenty days. This is related by al-Bukhari, Abu Dawud, and ibn-Majah. The Prophet's companions and wives performed *i'tikāf* with him and continued to do so after his death. Even though it is an act which is done to get closer to Allah, there is no sound *hadith* concerning its merits. Abu Dawud states: "I said to Ahmad, 'Are you aware of anything concerning the virtues of *i'tikāf*?' He answered: 'No, except for some weak [reports].' "

The different types of *i'tikāf*: *I'tikāf* is of two types: *sunnah* and obligatory. The *sunnah i'tikāf* is that which the Muslim performs to get closer to Allah by following the actions of the Prophet, upon whom be peace, especially during the last ten days of Ramadan. The obligatory *i'tikaf* is that which the person makes obligatory upon himself. This may be done, for example, by an oath: "For Allah I must make *i'tikaf*," or by a conditional oath: "If Allah cures me, I shall make *i'tikaf* . . ." In *Sahih al-Bukhari* it is reported that the Prophet, upon whom be peace, said: "Whoever makes an oath to obey Allah should be obedient to Him." 'Umar said: "O Messenger of Allah, I made an oath to perform *i'tikaf* one night in the mosque at Makkah." The Prophet, upon whom be peace, said: "Fulfill your oath."

The length of *i'tikaf*: The obligatory *i'tikaf* is to be as long as the oath states it to be. If one makes an oath to make *i'tikaf* for one day or more, he is to fulfill that length of time.

The *sunnah* or preferred *i'tikaf* has no specific time limit. It can be fulfilled by staying in the mosque with the intention of making *i'tikaf* for a long or short time. The reward will be according to how long one stays in the mosque. If one leaves the mosque and then returns, he should renew his intention to perform *i'tikaf*. Ya'la ibn Umayyah said: "I secluded myself in the mosque for some time for *i'tikaf*." 'Ata told him: "That is *i'tikaf*, as long as you secluded yourself there. If you sit in the mosque hoping for good, it is *i'tikaf*. Otherwise, it is not." One who is performing the nonobligatory *i'tikaf* may end his *i'tikaf* at any time, even if it is before the period he intended to stay. 'Aishah related that if the Prophet intended to make *i'tikaf*, he would pray the morning prayer and begin it. One time he wanted to make *i'tikaf* during the last ten nights of Ramadan, and he ordered his tent to be set up. Aishah reported: "When I saw that, I ordered my tent to be set up, and some of the Prophetesives followed suit. When he [the Prophet] prayed the morning prayer, he saw all of the tents, and said: "What is this?" They said: "We are seeking obedience [to Allah and His Messenger]." Then he ordered his tent and those of his wives to be taken down, and he delayed his *i'tikaf* to the first ten days [of Shawwal]." The fact that the messenger of Allah ordered his wives' tents to be struck down and asked them to leave the *i'tikaf* after they have made the intention for it shows that they discarded the *i'tikaf* after they had begun it. The *hadith* also shows that a man may prevent his wife from preforming *i'tikaf* if she did not get his permission to perform it. There is a difference of opinion over the case of the man granting permission to his wife and then rescinding it. According to ash-

Shaf'i, Ahmad, and Dawud, this is permissible for the husband, and the wife must leave her *i'tikaf* in such case.

The condition for *i'tikaf*: The one who preforms *i'tikaf* must be a Muslim adult , a discerning child who is free of sexual defilement, or an adolescent who is free of menstrual or childbirth bleeding. *i'tikaf* is not acceptable from an unbeliever, a non-discerning child, a sexually defiled person, a menstruating woman with post-childbirth bleeding.

The principles of *i'tikaf*: *I'tikaf* will be fulfilled if a person stays in the mosque with the intention of becoming closer to Allah. If the person is not in the mosque or did not do it with the intention to please Allah, it is not *i'tikaf*. The fact that the intention is obligatory is proven by Allah words: "They are ordained nothing else than to serve Allah, keeping religion pure for Him." The Prophet said: "Every action is according to the intention [behind it] and for everyone is what he intended."

Certainly, *i'tikaf* must be done in the mosque, as Allah says: "And do not touch and be at your devotions in the mosque [*al-Baqarah*: 178]." This *'ayah* proves that if it were proper for *i'tikaf* to be performed elsewhere, why would Allah exclusively disallow coming to one's wife during *i'tikaf*? The answer is that since such an act would nullify *i'tikaf* (no matter where it is peformed), it is clear that *i'tikaf* itself must be in the mosque.

The opinion of the jurists concerning the mosques in which the *i'tikaf* is to be performed: There is a difference of opinion among the jurists concerning what mosques are acceptable for *i'tikaf*. According to Abu Hanifah, Ahmad, Ishaq, and Abu Thaur, *i'tikaf* is valid in any mosque in which the five prayers are held and which has a congregation. This is based on the *hadith* of the Prophet: "Every mosque that has a caller to prayer and an *imam* is acceptable for *i'tikaf*." This is related by ad-Daraqutni, but the *hadith* is *mursal* and weak and cannot be used as a proof.

Malik, ash-Shaf'i, and Dawud say that it is acceptable in any mosque, as there is no proof that restricts it to any particular mosques. The Shaf'iyyah say it is better to perform *i'tikaf* in a congregational mosque, as the Prophet, upon whom be peace, performed *i'tikaf* in such a mosque, and because the number of those who attend the prayers in such a mosque is greater. If the period of *i'tikaf* includes the time for the Friday prayer, then one must perform it in the congregational mosque in order not to miss the Friday prayer.

The person making *i'tikaf* may make the call to prayer if the place from whence the call is made is either the door of the mosque or its interior courtyard. He may also go to the roof of the mosque, as all of that is considered part of the mosque. If the place for the call to prayer is outside of the mosque, and the *mu'takif* makes the call, he will void his *i'tikaf*. The exterior courtyard is considered part of the mosque according to the Hanafiyyah and Shaf'iyyah and one narration from Ahmad. According to Malik and another narration, it is not part of the mosque and the person making *i'tikaf* should not go there.

Most scholars say that it is not correct for a woman to make *i'tikaf* in the mosque in her house (that is, the special place of her house where she performs her prayers) because the mosque in her house usually does not fall in the category of mosques and can be sold. There is no difference of opinion on this point. The wives of the Prophet always performed their *i'tikaf* in the Prophet's mosque.

The Beginning and Ending of *i'tikaf*: We have already mentioned that the voluntary *i'tikaf* does not have any specific time period. Whenever a person enters the mosque and makes the intention of becoming closer to Allah by staying there, he will be peforming *i'tikaf* until he leaves. If he has the intention to perform *i'tikaf* during the last ten days of Ramadan, he should begin it before the sun sets. Al-Bukhari records from Abu Sa'id that the Prophet, upon whom be peace, said: "Whoever makes *i'tikaf* with me is to make *i'tikaf* during the last ten [nights]." The ten refers to the last ten nights which begin on the night of the 20th or the 21st.

Concerning the statement that when the Prophet desired to make *i'tikaf* he would pray the morning and then go to the place of his *i'tikaf*, it means that he used to enter the place which he had prepared for his seclusion, but the actual time that he entered the mosque for his seclusion was during the beginning of the night.

According to Abu Hanifah and ash-Shaf'i, whoever performs *i'tikaf* during the last ten days of Ramadan must leave the mosque after sunset on the last day of the month. Malik and Ahmad say that it is acceptable to leave after sunset, but they prefer for the person to remain in the mosque until the time for the *'id* prayer.

Al-'Athram records from Abu Ayyub that Abu Qulabah would stay in the mosque on the night before the *'id* prayer and would then go to the *'id* prayer. During his *i'tikaf*, he had no mat or prayer carpet to sit on. He used to sit like anyone else. Abu Ayyub said: "I came to him on the day of *'id* and on his lap was Juwairiyah Muzinah. I thought it was one of his daughters, but it was a slave that he had freed, and he came that way to the *'id* prayer." Ibrahim said: "The people preferred that one who performed *i'tikaf* during the last ten days of Ramadan stay in the mosque on the night of *'id* and then proceed to the *'id* prayer from the mosque.

If an individual makes a vow to perform *i'tikaf* for a specific period of days, or he wants to do so voluntarily, then he should begin his *i'tikaf* before dawn and leave when all the sun's light has gone, regardless of whether that be during Ramadan or at another time. If he vowed to perform *i'tikaf* for a night or a specified number of nights, or if he wants to do so voluntarily, then he should begin his *i'tikaf* before the sun has completely set and may leave when it is clear that dawn has begun. Ibn Hazm says: "The night begins when the sun sets and ends with dawn. The day begins with dawn and is completed by sunset. This is not a condition upon anyone unless he desires or intends to fulfill it. If one vows or wants to make *i'tikaf* voluntarily for a month, he should begin during the first night of the month. He should enter the mosque before the sun has completely set and may leave after the sun has completely set at the end of the month — regardless of whether it is Ramadan or otherwise."

What is preferred for the person who is fasting and what is disliked for him? It is preferred for the one who is making *i'tikaf* to perform many supererogatory acts of worship and to occupy himself with prayers, reciting the Qur'an, glorifying and praising Allah, extolling His oneness and His greatness, asking His forgiveness, sending salutations on the Prophet, upon whom be peace, and supplicating Allah — that is, all actions that bring one closer to Allah. Included among these actions is studying and reading books of *tafsir* and *hadith*, books on the lives of the Prophets, upon whom be peace, books of *fiqh*, and so on. It is also preferred to set up a small tent in the courtyard of the mosque as the Prophet did.

It is disliked for one to engage himself in affairs that do not concern him. At-Tirmidhi and Ibn Majah record on the authority of Abu Basrah that the Prophet said: "Part of a man's good observance of Islam is that he leave alone that which does not concern him." It is, however, disliked for a person to think that he can draw closer to Allah by not speaking. Al-Bukhari, Abu Dawud, and Ibn Majah record from Ibn 'Abbas that while the Prophet was delivering a speech, he saw a man standing and asked about him. The people said: "He is Abu Israel. He has vowed to stand and not to sit, and not to speak, and to fast." The Prophet said: "Order him to speak, go to the shade, to sit, and to complete his fast." Abu Dawud related from 'Ali that the Prophet said: "There is no orphanhood after one has passed the age of maturity, and there is no non-speaking for a day until the nightfall."

Fasting while performing *i'tikaf*: It is good for the person performing *i'tikaf* to fast, but he is not under any obligation to do so. Al-Bukhari records from Ibn 'Umar that 'Umar said: "O Messenger of Allah, during the days of ignorance I vowed to perform *i'tikaf* one night in the mosque at Makkah. The Prophet said: 'Fulfill your vow.'" This statement of the Prophet, upon whom be peace, shows that fasting is not a condition for *i'tikaf*; otherwise, performing *i'tikaf* at night would not be valid. Sa'id ibn Mansur records that Abu Sahl said: "One of my wives was to perform *i'tikaf*, so I asked 'Umar ibn 'Abdulaziz about it. He said: 'She need not fast, unless she imposes it upon herself.' Az-Zuhri said: 'There is no *i'tikaf* save while fasting.' 'Umar asked: 'Is this from the Prophet?' Az-Zuhri answered, 'No.' 'Umar asked, 'From Abu Bakr?' Az-Zuhri said,'No.' 'Umar asked [again], 'From 'Umar [ibn al-Khattab]?' Az-Zuhri said, 'No.' 'Umar said: 'I suspect he said it from 'Uthman?' Az-Zuhri said, 'No.' I [Abu Sahl] left them and met 'Ata and Tawus and asked them about it. Tawus said: 'A person would see that he did not have to fast unless he imposed it on himself.'"

Al-Khattabi acknowledges [the differences on the issue]: "There is a difference of opinion among the people on this point."

Al-Hassan al-Basri holds: "Performing *i'tikaf* without fasting suffices. That is also the opinion of ash-Shaf'i."

'Ali and Ibn Mas'ud maintain: "If one wishes, one may fast and if one does not wish to, one does not have to."

Al-Auza'i and Malik hold: "There is no *i'tikaf* without fasting, and that is the conclusion of the people of opinion. That has been related from Ibn 'Umar, Ibn 'Abbas, and 'Aishah, and it is the opinion of Sa'eed ibn al-Musayyeb, 'Urwah ibn az-Zubair, and az-Zuhri."

Permissible Acts for the *Mu'takif*

The following acts are permissible for one who is making *i'tikaf*:

(1) The person may leave his place of *i'tikaf* to bid farewell to his wife. Safiyyah reported: "The Prophet was performing *i'tikaf* and I went to visit him during the night. I talked to him and then I got up to go. He got up with me and accompanied me to my house. (Her residence was in the house of Usamah ibn Zaid. Two men of the Ansar passed by them and when they saw the Prophet they quickened their pace.) The Prophet said: 'Hold on, she is Safiyyah bint Haya.' They said: 'Glory be to Allah, O Messenger of Allah [we did not have any doubt about you].' The Prophet, upon whom be peace, said: 'Satan flows in the person like blood. I feared that he might have whispered some [slander] into your heart.'" This is related by al-Bukhari, Muslim, and Abu Dawud.

(2) Combing and cutting one's hair, clipping one's nails, cleaning one's body, wearing nice clothes or wearing perfume are all permissible. 'Aishah reported: "The Prophet was performing *i'tikaf* and he would put his head out through the opening to my room and I would clean [or comb in one narration] his hair. I was menstruating at the time." This is related by al-Bukhari, Muslim, and Abu Dawud.

(3) The person may go out for some need that he must perform. 'Aishah reported: "When the Prophet performed *i'tikaf*, he brought his head close to me so I could comb his hair, and he would not enter the house except to fulfill the needs a person has." This is related by al-Bukhari, Muslim, and others.

Ibn al-Mundhir says: "The scholars agree that the one who performs *i'tikaf* may leave the mosque in order to answer the call of nature, for this is something that he personally must perform, and he cannot do it in the mosque. Also, if he needs to eat or drink and there is no one to bring him his food, he may leave to get it. If one needs to vomit, he may leave the mosque to do so. For anything that he must do but cannot do in the mosque, he can leave it, and such acts will not void his *i'tikaf*, even if they take a long time. Examples of these types of acts would include washing one's self from sexual defilement and cleaning his body or clothes from impurities."

Sa'id ibn Mansur records that 'Ali said: "If a person is performing *i'tikaf*, he is to attend the Friday congregational prayer, be present at funerals, visit the ill and go to see his family about matters that are necesssary, but he is to remain standing [while visiting them]." 'Ali helped his nephew by giving him 700 dirhams to buy a servant and the nephew said: "I am performing *i'tikaf*". 'Ali said: "What blame would there be upon you if you go to the market to buy one?" Qatadah used to permit the person who was performing *i'tikaf* to follow the funeral procession and to visit the sick, but not to sit while doing so. Ibrahim an-Nakha'i says that they preferred that the person who was performing *i'tikaf* do the following deeds and he was allowed to do them even if he did not do them to visit the sick, to attend the Friday prayers, to witness the funerals, to go out to meet his needs, and not to enter a place that has a ceiling. He said: "The one who is performing *i'tikaf* should not enter a roofed place unless there is a need to do so." Al-Khattabi says: "A group of people say that the person performing *i'tikaf* may attend the Friday prayer, visit the ill, and witness funerals. This has been related from 'Ali, and it is the opinion of Sa'id ibn Jubair, al-Hassan al-Basri, and an-Nakha'i." Abu Dawud records from 'Aishah that the Prophet would visit the sick while performing *i'tikaf*. He would visit them without steering away from his path. It has also been related from her that it is *sunnah* for the person not to leave his place of *i'tikaf* and visit the sick. This means that the person is not to leave his place of *i'tikaf* with the sole intention of visiting the sick, but if he passes by him, he may ask about him provided it is not out of his way.

(4) The person may eat, drink, and sleep in the mosque, and he should also keep it clean. He may make contracts for marriage, buying, selling, and so on.

Actions that Nullify the *I'tikaf*

If a person performs one of the following acts, his *i'tikaf* will be nullified:

(1). Intentionally leaving the mosque without any need to do so, even if it is for just a short time. In such a case, one would not be staying in the mosque, which is one of the principles of *i'tikaf*.

(2) Abandoning belief in Islam, as this would nullify all acts of worship. If you ascribe a partner to Allah, your work will fail and you will be among the losers.

(3) Losing one's reason due to insanity or drunkenness, or the onset of menstruation or post-childbirth bleeding, all of which disqualifies a person for *i'tikaf*.

(4) Sexual intercourse. Allah says: "But touch them not [that is, your wives] and be at your devotions in the mosque."

However, one may touch his wife without there being any desires. One of the Prophet's wives would comb his hair while he was performing *i'tikaf*. As for kissing or touching due to desire, Abu Hanifah and Ahmad say that it is not desirable, for it leads to something that is forbidden for the one performing *i'tikaf*. However, it does not nullify it unless one ejaculates. Malik says that it nullifies the *i'tikaf*, for it is an illegal touch regardless of whether the person involved ejaculates or not. From ash-Shaf'i there are two reports that correspond to the two preceding opinions.

Ibn Rushd explains that: "The reason for their differences of opinion is [the (fact) that] if a word has more than one meaning, one being literal and the other figurative, does the word apply at one time to all of them or not? This is one of the types of words that have more than one meaning. Those who say that it carries both meanings interpret 'touch' in the *'ayah* . . . 'and touch them not and be at your devotions in the mosque' in the unrestrictive sense — that is, covering both sexual intercourse and also actions [of touching] that are less than that. Those who don't say it carries all of its meanings and they are the majority say that the *'ayah* points to sexual intercourse or to touching that is less than intercourse. If we say that it refers to sexual intercourse by consensus, then this nullifies the possibility of it referring to actions less than intercourse, as one [single] word could not be taken in its literal and figurative meaning [at the same time]. Those who say that what is less than sexual intercourse is included say so because it falls under the literal meaning of the verse. Those who differ do not take the word in its literal and figurative meaning at the same time.

Making Up *I'tikaf*

If an individual intends to perform a voluntary *i'tikaf* and then ends it before he completes it, he should make up that *i'tikaf* later. Some say that it is obligatory to do so.

Writing on the subject, at-Tirmidhi says: "There is a difference of opinion about a person who ends his *i'tikaf* before his intended time has expired." Malik holds: "If he ends his *i'tikaf* [early], it is obligatory upon him to make it up. He uses as proof the *hadith* which states that when the Prophet abandoned his *i'tikaf*, he made it up during the following month of Shawwal." Ash-Shaf'i states: "If he did not vow to perform *i'tikaf* or he did not make it obligatory upon himself, and then he left it early, he does not have to make it up unless he chooses to do so." He continues: "One does not have to undertake this act. If he did and then left it, he need not make it up [since it was voluntary], except for the case of *hajj* and *'umrah*." Notwithstanding this, the *imams* agree that if one makes a vow to perform *i'tikaf* for a day or a number of days and then voids his *i'tikaf*, it is obligatory upon him to make it up whenever he can. If he dies before he makes it up, then no one is obliged to make it up on his behalf. On the other hand, Ahmad argues: "It is obligatory on his inheritors to make it up on his behalf. 'Abdurrazzaq related from 'Abdulkarim ibn Umayyah who said he heard 'Abdullah ibn 'Abdullah ibn 'Utbah say: "Our mother died while she still had some *i'tikaf* to perform. I asked Ibn 'Abbas and he said: 'Perform *i'tikaf* on her behalf and fast.' " Sa'id ibn Mansur recorded that 'Aishah performed *i'tikaf* on behalf of her brother after his death.

Retiring of the *Mu'takif to the Mosque and Setting Up of a Tent*

Ibn Majah recorded from Ibn 'Umar that the Prophet made *i'tikaf* during the last ten days of Ramadan. Nafi' reported: "Ibn 'Umar showed me the place where the Prophet would perform his *i'tikaf*."

He also reported that when the Prophet performed *i'tikaf*, he would spread out his bed behind the repentance pole (that is, the pole that a companion had tied himself to until Allah accepted his repentance).

Abu Sa'id reported that the Prophet performed *i'tikaf* under a Turkish tent which had something over its openings.

Making a Vow to Perform *I'tikaf* in a Specific Mosque

If someone makes a vow to perform *i'tikaf* in the Masjid al-Haram (in Makkah), the Prophet's Mosque (in Madinah), or in the Aqsa Mosque (in Jerusalem), he is to fulfill his vow, as the Prophet said: "One should not undertake journeys except to three mosques: the Masjid al-Haram, the Aqsa mosque, or this mosque."

If someone vows to perform *i'tikaf* in another mosque, it is not obligatory on him to fulfill it and he may perform that *i'tikaf* in any mosque, for Allah did not specify any particular place for His worship, and there is no superiority of one mosque over another (with the exception of the three mosques mentioned earlier). It has been confirmed that the Prophet said: "A prayer in my mosque is superior to one thousand prayers in any other mosque but the Masjid al-Haram, and a prayer in that mosque is superior to a prayer in my mosque by one hundred prayers."

Thus, if someone makes a vow to perform *i'tikaf* in the Prophet's mosque, he may fulfill it in the Masjid al-Haram since that one is superior to the Prophet's mosque.

INDEX

CPSIA information can be obtained
at www.ICGtesting.com
Printed in the USA
BVHW031201100121
597491BV00026B/301

9 780892 590667